Valentina's
ITALIAN FAMILY FEAST

Valentina's
ITALIAN FAMILY FEAST

Festive cooking for family occasions

VALENTINA HARRIS

Special photography by
Jacqui Hurst

CONRAN OCTOPUS

For B.J.W. – one of life's great givers

First published in 1990 by
Conran Octopus Limited
37 Shelton Street
London WC2H 9HN

Quantities in the recipes are given in
both metric and imperial. Use either all metric or
all imperial as they are not interchangeable.
Spoon measures are level unless otherwise stated.

British Library Cataloguing in Publication Data

Harris, Valentina
Valentina's Italian family feast.
1. Italy. Cookery
I. Title
641.50945

Art Director	Mary Evans
Art Editor	Peter Cross
Editor	Denise Bates
Copy Editor	Norma MacMillan
Picture Research	Nadine Bazar
Production	Sonya Sibbons
Italian Photographic Co-ordinator	Ian Rooks
Home Economist	Valerie Barrett

ISBN 1 85029 288 4

Typeset by Litho Link Limited, Welshpool, Powys, Wales
Printed in Italy

CONTENTS

INTRODUCTION
6

GOOD FRIDAY
8

EASTER SUNDAY
16

A RUSTIC LUNCH
24

GIUSEPPE'S NAME DAY
32

TUSCAN PICNIC
40

DINNER WITH ELEONORA
46

A BARBECUE IN RONCHI
54

CHIC MILANESE LUNCH
62

EATING ON THE BEACH
70

WEDDING ANNIVERSARY
DINNER
76

A FEAST OF RICOTTA
84

A WEDDING IN SICILY
92

SEAFOOD LUNCH
102

JUST A PARTY
110

MARIA'S
VENETIAN BIRTHDAY
118

SUNDAY LUNCH
IN THE GARDEN
126

CHRISTMAS EVE FEAST
132

INDEX
AND ACKNOWLEDGMENTS
142

INTRODUCTION

This is the book about Italian food that I have always wanted to write. The idea behind it was to give the reader an insight into what Italian food is *really* about – celebration! And there seemed no better way to show how rooted Italian cookery is in the simple enjoyment of good food in good company than with my own family and friends.

In the course of collecting these authentic recipes Jacqui, the photographer, and I travelled the length and breadth of Italy, calling in on friends and relatives and inviting ourselves to special and everyday occasions alike. The book is completely different from anything else I have written, because it is concerned with absolute spontaneity. The photographs and recipes are what was actually cooked and eaten on the day itself, there is not a single studio picture anywhere.

The sections of the book are divided into menus which give a very good idea of how to combine the various flavours and textures.

It is just these combinations which can make beautifully simple Italian food also delightfully complex and this is one of the principles I set out to put across in the chapters which follow.

There were so many willing friends who became involved in the putting together of this book – to all of them, I would like to express my deepest thanks. In particular, I would like to thank Ferruccio Nobile Migliore for all the shopping and preparation, Leonora Carpi for her contacts and Maurizio for entertaining us so well in Perugia. I would also like to say a very big thank you to the Gelmetti family in Lodi for helping me out again and feel I should apologize for waking them so early on a Sunday morning! My thanks and affection also go to Eleonora Consoli, and to Katia Fongoli. It is wonderful to be reminded that the spirit of hospitality and the joy of sharing are still alive and well in Italian families. Last, but by no means least, thank you to Ian and Edward.

RUSTIC TABLE (right) *Tree trunks provide the legs for this laden table on a farm in Sicily.*

ROME IN THE RAIN (right) *Customers are rather sparse at these market stalls in central Rome.*

IL VENERDÌ SANTO

Good Friday

When I was a little girl growing up in Italy, eating meat on Fridays was absolutely *never* done. Fridays were always taken up with trips to the fish stall and the subsequent preparation of whatever fish looked freshest. Only very rough seas could prevent the fishermen from supplying Friday's meal – in this case we had to eat dried salt cod or stockfish. Although I have come to appreciate the flavour of dried fish, at seven it was rather hard to stomach.

Later on the Pope changed all that. I know a few very religious Catholics who still persist in eating only fish on a Friday, but for almost everyone else things have relaxed considerably. Good Friday, however, is still the day when meat is never served and fish is the central part of the meal.

This is not a day for celebration – it is a sombre occasion in Italy, with the church bells tolling steadily in the villages. However,

as it is a national holiday, many families find themselves gathered together and so despite the seriousness of the day, there *is* a hint of enjoyment in the air.

As we were in Rome for Easter, I very much wanted to eat the traditional Roman *frittata del Venerdì Santo*, which is a lettuce omelette flavoured with sweet wine. I know it sounds odd, but it is in fact delicious, and, like so many other traditional recipes, in danger of disappearing. Ferruccio made his superb *ravioli di pesce* and served the clear soup in which the fish had been poached as a very light starter. This may not sound to everyone's taste, but in fact the soup is a marvellous way to begin the meal – it's known as an *apristomaco*, or stomach opener! For the ravioli he used the most deliciously fine dough.

As a main course, Ferruccio had chosen two different types of fish from his favourite and trusted

FISH SHOP (right) *Once a day of fasting and abstinence, Good Friday is still the day when fish, and never meat, is traditionally eaten.*

FERRUCIO'S DINING ROOM (right) *Our Good Friday lunch in Rome had a suitably splendid setting in Ferrucio's apartment.*

market stall. We had fillets of sole cooked with butter and oranges and then a much more dramatic and imposing dorade baked in the oven with olives. Leonora had bought mounds of purple-headed artichokes and brilliant, emerald-green fresh peas to serve as the main vegetable with the fish.

Dessert was in the form of *la pastiera*, an amazing cake whose origins date back to Ancient Rome. It was first prepared at this time of year to celebrate spring-time and fertility, which explains why it is made with wheat grain! Over the centuries, the Neapoli-tans have adopted it as their traditional Easter cake and nowa-days it can be bought in *pasticcerie* at Easter time. However, I can assure you that the *pastiera* you buy in Naples is completely dif-ferent to any version of the cake made elsewhere. The one we ate was home-made and very special, but there is a small Neapolitan pastry shop near the Opera House in Rome which makes them almost as well. If you do make the cake at home, make sure the grain has been soaked very thoroughly, and do remember to change the water frequently during the days the grain is soaking to prevent it from sprouting.

Menu

Brodo di Pesce

Ravioli di Pesce

Frittata del Venerdì Santo

Orata alle Olive

Carciofi e Pisellini alla Romana

Filetti di Sogliola all'Arancia

La Pastiera

BRODO DI PESCE

Fish Broth

SERVES 6

*1 kg (2¼ lb) assorted fish, amongst which there
should be some of the following: red mullet, grey
mullet, dentice, sea bass, cod and hake
1 small onion, quartered
2 sticks celery, quartered
3 sprigs of fresh parsley
2 sprigs of fresh rosemary
1 small lemon, sliced
salt
2 wineglasses of dry white wine*

Clean and wash the various fish or pieces of
fish. Lay them in a fairly deep saucepan and
put the vegetables, herbs and lemon on top.
Sprinkle generously with salt and pour in the
wine. Cover sparingly with water and bring to
the boil. Simmer, covered, for about 40
minutes to 1 hour. Remove from the heat and
take the fish out of the broth.

To make a very thick soup, take all the flesh
off the fish and purée it in a mouli or food
processor, then stir it back into the broth.

For clear fish broth, strain the liquid carefully, discarding the vegetables, herbs and
lemon, and heat to just below boiling. The
flesh of the fish can be used in another recipe,
for example the one following.

You can also use the broth to make delicious
fish risotto, or add it to fishy pasta sauces. Or
boil tiny pasta in the broth to make a
nourishing and simple soup.

FRESH FISH *Ferruccio invariably buys fish at a local
market stall he knows he can rely on.*

RAVIOLI DI PESCE

Fish Ravioli

SERVES 6

Pasta
500 g (1 lb 2 oz) plain flour
5 eggs (size 2)
a pinch of salt
½ teaspoon olive oil

Filling
⅔ of the fish from brodo di pesce (see p.10)
5 tablespoons ricotta cheese
2 tablespoons chopped fresh parsley
a pinch of grated nutmeg
salt and freshly milled pepper

Dressing
75 g (2½ oz) unsalted butter, melted but not
browned

Make the pasta first: sift the flour on to the work top, make a hole in the centre with your fist and put the eggs into the hole. Add the salt and oil and blend everything together with your fingertips. Knead together very thoroughly until you have a ball of smooth, elastic dough. Begin to roll it out, then fold it in half and roll it out again. Continue to do this until you hear the air pop out from the fold as you press down with the rolling pin. At this point the dough is ready to fill.

Roll it out one last time, as thinly as possible, and cut it all into rounds of about 6 cm (2½ in) in diameter with a pastry cutter or overturned glass. Leave the rounds on the work top while you quickly make the filling. (Don't leave them too long or they'll dry out and won't seal properly.)

Mash or purée the flesh from the fish and

After cutting out the pasta rounds, fill and seal them quickly so that they do not dry out.

RAVIOLI DI PESCE (left), BRODO DI PESCE (right)

mix it with all the other filling ingredients. Arrange small teaspoonfuls in the centre of each pasta round. Fold the rounds in half and press them tightly closed with the prongs of a fork, making little grooves along the edge.

Toss the ravioli into a large pot of boiling salted water and cook them for about 2 or 3 minutes. Scoop them out carefully with a slotted spoon then cover with the melted butter and serve.

FRITTATA DEL VENERDÌ SANTO

Good Friday Omelette

SERVES 6–8

100 ml (3½ fl oz) olive oil
2 onions, chopped
1 head of cos lettuce, trimmed, washed and finely
chopped
a handful of rocket, washed and chopped
3 tablespoons vin santo or other sweet wine
salt and freshly milled pepper
10 eggs, beaten
5 tablespoons freshly grated Parmesan cheese, or 3
tablespoons Parmesan and 2 tablespoons freshly
grated pecorino cheese

Heat half the oil in a wide pan, and put all the vegetables into the oil. Cook until soft over a medium heat, turning frequently. Add the wine and boil to evaporate the fumes for 2–3 minutes, then season with plenty of salt and freshly milled pepper.

Beat the eggs with the cheese and season with salt and pepper. Heat the remaining oil in a large frying pan until sizzling. Mix the vegetables into the egg and cheese mixture, then quickly tip this into the hot oil. Spread out in an even layer and cook until set and golden brown on the bottom, shaking the pan frequently to prevent the omelette from sticking too much.

If using a non-stick pan, turn the omelette out on to a big plate or lid, then slide it back into the pan the other way up. Cook the other side until well browned. Otherwise, leave the omelette in the pan and cook the top under a hot grill. Serve hot or cold.

ORATA ALLE OLIVE

Baked Dorade with Olives

SERVES 6

*1 or 2 whole dorade (gilt-head bream) or similar
fish, total weight about 2 kg (4½ lb), gutted
8 tablespoons olive oil
100g (3½ oz) green olives, stoned
150 g (5 oz) black olives, stoned
4 cloves garlic, coarsely chopped
4 bay leaves, coarsely chopped
4 sprigs of fresh rosemary, coarsely chopped
salt*

Wash and dry the fish thoroughly. Pull the
spine away from the flesh as much as possible
by inserting the point of a knife under the bone
and pulling outwards. Fill the fish and cover it
with the olives. Sprinkle the garlic, bay leaves,
rosemary and salt over and inside the fish.
Place in an oiled baking dish and drizzle the oil
over the fish.

Place the dish in a baking tin containing
enough water to come halfway up the sides of
the dish. Bake in a preheated moderate oven
(180°C, 350°F, gas mark 4) for about 35
minutes or until the fish will flake easily when
tested with a skewer. Serve hot.

OLIVES AND SPRIGS OF ROSEMARY *The flavour of
fresh rosemary blends beautifully with olives.*

CARCIOFI E PISELLINI ALLA ROMANA

Roman Artichokes with Peas

SERVES 6

6 large globe artichokes
1 large lemon, quartered
1 large onion, chopped
4 slices of prosciutto crudo, very finely chopped
5 tablespoons olive oil
3 sprigs of fresh mint, finely chopped
3 cloves garlic, chopped
salt and freshly milled pepper
300 g (11 oz) shelled fresh peas

Cut all the outside layers off the artichokes and trim off sharp points. Cut the artichokes in half and remove the furry choke. Soak in a basin of cold water with the lemon quarters for about 30 minutes.

Put the onion and prosciutto into a deep, wide frying pan and begin to fry gently together. Add the oil, mint and garlic and cook for a further 5 minutes.

Drain the artichokes and add them to the pan. Season. Cover and cook for about 15 minutes, occasionally pouring a little water over the artichokes to prevent them drying out and stirring from time to time. When they are fairly tender, add the peas and cook for a further 10 minutes or until both vegetables are completely tender. Serve hot or cold.

FILETTI DI SOGLIOLA ALL'ARANCIA

Fillets of Sole with Orange

SERVES 6–8

75 g (2½ oz) unsalted butter
12 fillets of sole
grated rind and juice of 1 orange
salt

Melt the butter in 2 wide frying pans and cook the fillets of sole gently in the butter for 2 minutes on each side. Reserve the juices and put the fish on a dish to keep warm.

Combine the fish juices in one pan and add the orange juice, grated rind and seasoning. Heat, pour all over the fish and serve.

CARCIOFI E PISELLINI ALLA ROMANA

FILETTI DI SOGLIOLA ALL'ARANCIA

LA PASTIERA

Traditional Neapolitan Easter Cake

For this recipe you need wheat which has been soaked in cold water for about 8 days.

MAKES ONE *30 CM (12 IN) CAKE*

Filling
approx 180 g (6 oz) dried wheat
500 ml (18 fl oz) milk
pared rind of ½ lemon
2 large pinches of ground cinnamon
200 g (7 oz) granulated sugar
2 teaspoons vanilla essence
500 g (1 lb 2 oz) freshest possible ricotta cheese
grated rind of ½ lemon
3 tablespoons orange flower water
90 g (3½ oz) candied orange and lime, very finely chopped
6 egg yolks
4 egg whites
Pastry
300 g (11 oz) plain flour
150 g (5 oz) freshest possible lard
150 g (5 oz) sugar
3 egg yolks
To Finish
lard for greasing
1 egg, beaten
icing sugar for dusting

Soak the wheat in cold water for 8 days in a cool place. Change the water at least once a day during this time. At the end of the 8 days, drain and rinse the grain very thoroughly. Weigh out 250 g (9 oz) and discard the rest.

LA PASTIERA

Put the weighed grain in a saucepan. Bring the milk to the boil in another pan, then pour it all over the grain. Add the pared lemon rind, a pinch of cinnamon and a heaped tablespoon of the sugar. Stir well. Simmer for about 2 hours on the lowest possible heat.

While the grain cooks, make the pastry. Sift the flour on to the work top in a pile, make a hole in the centre, and put the lard, sugar and egg yolks into the hole. Blend all these ingredients together very quickly with your fingertips (or in a food processor) to make a smooth dough. Do not knead the dough: work it only for the time it takes to make an amalgamated mass. Wrap the ball of dough and rest in the fridge for about 30 minutes.

When the grain has absorbed all the liquid and is just falling apart, take it off the heat and leave to cool completely in the covered pan.

Sieve the ricotta into a bowl and add the rest of the sugar, cinnamon, the grated lemon rind, orange flower water and candied fruit. Mix together lightly, then add the egg yolks *one at a time*, making sure each one is well blended in before you add another. Whisk the egg whites until stiff. Stir in the cooled grain, then fold in the egg whites.

Grease a deep 30 cm (12 in) cake tin generously with lard. Roll out about two–thirds of the pastry dough and use to line the tin. Pour the ricotta filling into the centre and smooth it out carefully. Roll out the remaining pastry dough and cut into strips. Use to make a lattice pattern on the filling, anchoring the strips securely to the edges of the pastry case. Brush the pastry with beaten egg. Bake in a preheated oven (180°C, 350°F, gas mark 4) for 1 hour or until golden brown and firm to the touch. Let the cake cool in the tin, then sprinkle it generously with sifted icing sugar. The cake is better eaten a few days after baking.

LA PASQUA

Easter Sunday

As a complete contrast to Good Friday, Easter Sunday really is about celebrating. The most devout will have been to church at midnight on Saturday, so the whole of Sunday can be given over to being with one's family and to the sheer indulgent enjoyment of the main feast.

Everybody always has lamb (or kid) on Easter Sunday in Italy, cooked in many different ways. In some households it is cooked over an open fire on a spit or very large grill, whilst others will braise it with vegetables or make some kind of stew. Whatever is done with it, for many families in the north of Italy this is the only day of the year when lamb is eaten – although of course this doesn't apply to the south, where it is virtually the only meat that is widely cooked.

For anybody who still had room after the main courses, we had the traditional savoury *torta pasqualina* – the Ligurian Easter cake made with 33 layers, one for each year of Christ's life, and finally a *colomba,* the dove-shaped Easter cake that is sold all over Italy but which can also be made at home if you feel so inclined. When I was a child you could only buy the plain kind with almond and sugar topping, but nowadays they come with all kinds of fillings and icings and frostings, from champagne mousse to strawberry jelly. Take a tip from me, however – the old-fashioned one is by far the nicest!

When everybody was absolutely full up, it was time to allow the children to dive into the colourfully wrapped chocolate Easter eggs, in which a present, usually a toy, is hidden. The egg hunt then took over for the rest of the afternoon. My mother hides painted eggs for her grandchildren, just as she always hid them for us when we were young, and there seemed to be such a lot of eggs, hidden on the handlebars of bicycles, in the forks of trees, under lettuces in the vegetable garden and in a thousand and one other places which are used year after year. There have to be lots of eggs, otherwise the whole thing would be over in minutes! As nobody ever bothers to count how many eggs have been hidden, the hunt is over when no more can be found. The funny thing is, we then spend the following fortnight discovering more eggs hidden all over the garden . . .

Menu

Lasagnette con Spinaci e Funghi

Agnello Braciato

Fave in Purè

Patate Arrosto

Carote al Latte

La Torta Pasqualina

La Colomba

EASTER EGGS (left) *Hidden inside each lavishly wrapped chocolate egg is a present, usually a toy.*

OPENING THE EGGS (left) *With my excited children the usual result is a lot of broken chocolate!*

LASAGNETTE CON SPINACI E FUNGHI

Lasagnette with Spinach and Mushrooms

SERVES 6

500 g (1lb 2 oz) fresh spinach
150 g (5 oz) butter
salt and freshly milled pepper
25 g (1 oz) dried funghi porcini, *soaked in warm*
water for 10 minutes and rinsed well
500 g (1lb 2 oz) lasagnette
8 tablespoons cream
75 g (2½ oz) Parmesan cheese, freshly grated

Wash the spinach, then cook it in 2 or 3 tablespoons of water until it is just soft. Squeeze it dry with your hands, then chop it finely with a sharp knife. Put the spinach in a pan with half the butter and sauté it briefly for just 2 or 3 minutes.

Bring a large pot of salted water to the boil. Drain the mushrooms, chop them finely and add them to the spinach. Mix the spinach and mushrooms together over a low heat. Season to taste. Remove from the heat and keep the vegetables warm.

When the water boils, toss in the lasagnette and boil until *al dente* (check packet for timing as brands vary).

Drain the pasta and tip it into a warmed bowl. Add the warm spinach and mushroom mixture, the rest of the butter and the cream. Toss everything together very thoroughly and season well.

Sprinkle with the Parmesan and toss once more before serving.

AGNELLO BRACIATO

Braised Lamb

SERVES 6

85 g (3 oz) butter
4 tablespoons sunflower oil
1 leg of lamb, boned weight about 2 kg (4½ lb)
1 large onion, thickly sliced
1 large carrot, coarsely chopped
2 large sticks celery, coarsely chopped
a handful of fresh parsley, coarsely chopped
salt and freshly milled pepper
2 large wineglasses of dry white wine
500 ml (¾ pint) broth or stock

Heat half the butter with the oil in a deep flameproof casserole for 2 or 3 minutes, then seal the leg of lamb all over in the hot fat, browning it well. Remove the lamb and wrap in foil to keep warm. Put all the vegetables and the parsley into the casserole and cook gently until soft and golden brown. Add a little water if they begin to get too brown or stick to the casserole. When the vegetables are cooked, return the meat to the casserole with any juices which have leaked out into the foil. Season.

Add a little wine, and boil to evaporate the fumes for 3 minutes. Continue in this way until all the wine has been added. Add the broth or stock a little at a time, turning the meat each time and allowing the liquid to evaporate before you add any more. This takes about 1½ hours – make sure you keep the heat low and let the meat cook slowly.

When the meat is ready, it will be well browned and coated in a glossy brown sauce. Remove the meat from the casserole and slice it carefully. Arrange the slices on a warm platter. Add a little more wine or stock to the sauce in the casserole and bring it to the boil, stirring. Add the rest of the butter and stir until melted, then pour this sauce over the sliced meat. Serve at once.

LAMB ON A SPIT (left) *Some families roast their Easter lamb on a spit over the open fire.*

FAVE IN PURÈ

Purée of Broad Beans

SERVES 6

1.5 kg (3¼ lb) fresh broad beans in their pods, or frozen broad beans
salt and freshly milled pepper
150 ml (¼ pint) cream
100 g (3½ oz) butter
1 teaspoon caster sugar

Shell the broad beans and remove their tough inner skins. This may seem time-consuming but it really enhances the taste. Rinse them carefully. Cook in boiling salted water for about 5 minutes (frozen beans need about 12 minutes). Drain the beans and push them through a mouli or whizz in a food processor to make a smooth purée.

Return the purée to the saucepan and heat gently, stirring constantly. Add the cream a little at a time, still stirring, then add the butter and caster sugar. Finally, season to taste with salt and freshly milled pepper, and serve the purée piping hot.

(left to right) CAROTE AL LATTE, PATATE ARROSTO, AGNELLO BRACIATO

PATATE ARROSTO

Roast Potatoes

SERVES 6

500 g (18 oz) potatoes suitable for roasting
150 ml (¼ pint) sunflower oil
3 cloves garlic
salt and freshly milled pepper

Peel the potatoes and cut them into equal-sized 4 cm (1½ in) chunks. Part-cook them in boiling salted water for 2–3 minutes, then drain. Heat the oil with the peeled garlic in a preheated moderately hot oven (200°C, 400°F, gas mark 6) until the garlic turns golden brown. Remove the roasting tin from the oven and add the potatoes. Season generously and turn the potatoes so they are coated all over with the garlic-flavoured oil. Spread the potatoes out evenly in the tin.

Return to the oven to roast until crisp and golden brown. This should take about 45 minutes. Serve very hot.

LEAVING CHURCH ON SUNDAY MORNING *It is a tradition on Easter Sunday morning to take food to the church to be blessed.*

CAROTE AL LATTE

Carrots in Milk

SERVES 6

750 g (1 lb 11 oz) carrots, sliced into rounds
salt and freshly milled pepper
15 g (½ oz) butter
200 ml (7 fl oz) milk
1 egg yolk

Bring a saucepan of salted water to the boil, toss in the carrots and cook for 5 minutes. Drain the carrots and put them in a large pan with the butter and three-quarters of the milk. Season to taste. Cook for a further 6 or 7 minutes, or until tender. Season well. Add the rest of the milk and the egg yolk and stir quickly together to thicken the sauce. Watch the sauce carefully and as soon as it thickens transfer everything to a warmed dish and serve immediately.

LA TORTA PASQUALINA

Ligurian Easter Pie

SERVES 10–12

1 kg (2¼ lb) frozen filo pastry, defrosted (you will need 18–33 sheets, large enough to cover the bottom of a 30 cm/12 in cake tin)
12 globe artichokes, as young and tender as possible
1 onion, finely sliced
juice of 1 lemon
75 ml (3 fl oz) olive oil
salt and freshly milled pepper
4 slices of stale white bread, crusts removed
150 ml (5 fl oz) milk
10 eggs, as fresh as possible
8 heaped tablespoons freshly grated Parmesan cheese
600 g (1¼ lb) ricotta or whipped cream cheese
melted butter or oil for brushing pastry
100 g (3½ oz) unsalted butter, finely diced
1 tablespoon chopped fresh marjoram

Prepare the artichokes (see p.13). Cut each artichoke in half, remove the choke with a teaspoon and slice the artichoke. Put the slices

LA TORTA PASQUALINA (right)

in a saucepan immediately with the onion, lemon juice and about 5 tablespoons of olive oil. Cook gently for about 20 minutes, stirring frequently. Season with salt and pepper.

While the artichokes are cooking, soak the bread for 10 minutes in the milk, in a large bowl. In another bowl, beat 4 eggs with 3 tablespoons of the grated Parmesan. Stir this mixture into the bread and milk. Add the cooked artichokes, then the ricotta. Mix very thoroughly, then set to one side until required.

Oil a 30 cm (12 in) cake tin, which needs to be fairly deep, preferably about 13 cm (5 in). Lay the first sheet of pastry on the bottom of the cake tin and brush it with butter. Continue to layer the sheets in the tin, brushing each one with butter before you put in the next one. On the 11th sheet, spread the artichoke filling. Using the back of a spoon, make 6 little hollows in the surface of the filling. Put a tiny piece of unsalted butter in each hollow, then break an egg on top of the butter, being very careful not to break the yolk. Cover each egg with grated Parmesan, and sprinkle with salt, pepper and marjoram. Lay the next sheet of pastry over the filling, brush it with butter and dot a little unsalted butter all around the edge. Lay in another sheet, brush it with butter and dot unsalted butter around the edges. Continue in this way until you have used up all the pastry. Any pastry which hangs over the edge of the tin must be folded back and pressed down lightly to create a thicker band around the edge of the pie. When cooked it will give you a very crisp crust.

Pierce holes with a skewer all over the surface of the pie, then brush very thoroughly with butter. Place in a preheated moderately hot oven (190°C, 375°F, gas mark 5) and bake for 1 hour. Serve tepid or cold, as part of a buffet or for a special occasion picnic.

LA COLOMBA

Easter Dove Cake

MAKES ONE 25 CM (10 IN) CAKE

1.2 kg (2½ lb) plain flour
50 g (1¾ oz) fresh yeast
8 egg yolks
a pinch of salt
grated rind of 1 lemon
400 g (14 oz) unsalted butter
300 g (11 oz) granulated sugar
120 ml (4 fl oz) milk
300 g (11 oz) mixed candied fruit, chopped
100 g (3½ oz) sultanas
1 egg, beaten
2–3 tablespoons sugar crystals

Set aside about 200 g (7 oz) of flour, for dusting the work surface and flouring your hands.

Pour 2 litres (3½ pints) of water into a deep saucepan and warm until just tepid. Crumble the yeast into a large bowl, add about 50 ml (1¾ fl oz) of tepid water and blend together. Mix in 120 g (4 oz) of plain flour, making a dry, firm dough. Roll this up into a ball. Drop this ball into the tepid water and leave it there for 10 minutes, at which point it should rise up to the surface. Turn it over and leave it floating for 15 minutes, turning it over occasionally.

Meanwhile, put the remaining flour, minus the quantity set aside, into a very large mixing bowl (3 times the size of the ball the dough). Add to it the 8 egg yolks, the pinch of salt, grated lemon rind, about 200 g (7 oz) of butter, the sugar, the milk and the ball of dough which has been floating in water. Flour your hands and knead all this very thoroughly. If necessary, add a little more milk and flour from the quantity set aside and work at the dough until it is no longer sticky.

When it is completely smooth and elastic, put the dough into a bowl and place it in a warm place (about 25°C/77°F) to rise. (Beware of draughts.) When it has risen by one third, take it out and knock it back, then add about 100 g (3½ oz) of butter. Knead thoroughly, working in more flour if necessary, then return to the bowl in the warm place. When it has again risen by one third, knock it back and add in the remaining butter (saving enough for greasing), the candied fruit and sultanas.

Butter a 25 cm (10 in) deep cake tin, then put in the dough. Cover with greaseproof paper and allow the dough to rise for 30 minutes. Then remove the paper and cover the surface with egg and sugar crystals. Let the dough rest for 5 minutes, then bake in a preheated oven (190°C, 375°F, gas mark 5) for 10 minutes. Lower the heat to 180°C, 350°F, gas mark 4 and cover the cake with greaseproof paper again to prevent it browning too much. Bake for 1–1¼ hours or until a wooden cocktail stick inserted into the cake comes out clean. Cool on a wire rack.

PAINTED EGGS (above) *for the egg hunt.*
LA COLOMBA (right)

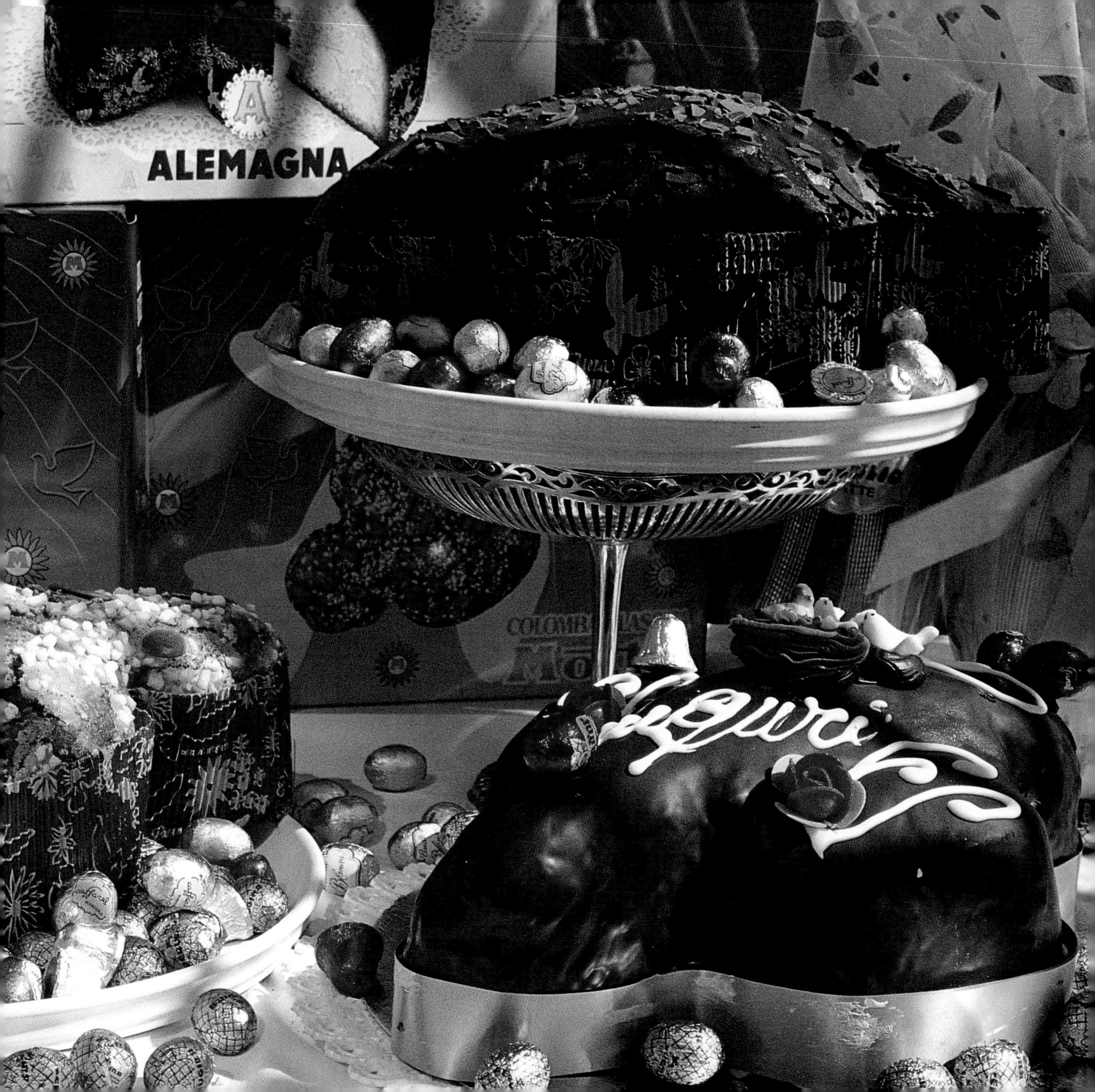
ALEMAGNA
Auguri

UN PRANZO MOLTO RUSTICO

A Rustic Lunch

Probably the most vital aspect of all Italian cuisine is *la cucina povera*, the peasant cuisine from which so much of Italian cooking sprang. This is food made with ingredients and to recipes which have changed very little over the centuries, despite the changes in Italy's economy. By and large, it aims at filling bellies while being as tasty and nourishing as possible, and because it was born out of necessity and local availability, there are absolutely no rigid rules – you can adapt and add your own touches as you like.

Probably the most enduring combination is that of pasta with the simplest of tomato sauces. Particularly in the south, large periods of time during August and September are dedicated to bottling fresh tomato sauce for the winter months. When I was a child we used to do this out in the garden: all those who had been enlisted for the job crouched around an old tin bath placed over

an open fire, with the bottles of tomatoes, wrapped tightly in newspaper, being boiled in the bath. It was incredibly hot work, and the mountains of overripe tomatoes never appeared to get any smaller. It seemed incredibly cruel sometimes, to be stuck at home doing this when the late summer sea with its great foaming waves was beckoning. But in February, when the rain was horizontal and the damp inescapable, it was just like having sunshine on your plate when the bottles were opened and the fragrant sauces poured out.

Menu

Minestra di Pasta e Broccoli

Pezzelle di Pane

Cappuccio Imbottito

Maltagliati al Sugo di Pomodoro

Rognone di Vitello alla Furnacella

Albanesi

MALTAGLIATI AL SUGO DI POMODORO (right), *eaten directly from the traditional wooden trough.*

RUSTIC STOREHOUSE (right) *These traditional utensils have changed little over the centuries.*

MINESTRA DI PASTA E BROCCOLI

Broccoli and Pasta Soup

SERVES 6

100 g (3½ oz) bacon fat, lard or ham fat
2 cloves garlic, finely chopped
½ dried red chilli pepper
1 bunch light green broccoli, weighing about 150 g
(5 oz) cut into very small florets
100 ml (3½ fl oz) dry white wine
750 ml (1¼ pints) cold water
salt and freshly milled pepper
300 g (11 oz) cannolicchietti or tiny Ave Marie
(very small pasta suitable for soups)
freshly grated pecorino cheese to taste

Fry the fat with the garlic and chilli until golden brown and sizzling. Add the broccoli and wine and cook for about 3 minutes, then add the water and cover the pan. Simmer for about 12 minutes or until the broccoli is tender, adding more water as required. Season with plenty of salt and pepper.

As soon as the broccoli is cooked, tip in the pasta and cook until it is *al dente*. Add plenty of freshly grated pecorino cheese to taste and serve hot, tepid or cold.

BOTTLED VEGETABLES (right) *Abundant summer vegetables are preserved and eaten as antipasti during the sparser winter months.*

PEZZELLE DI PANE

Baked Dry Bread with Cheese

SERVES 4–6

4 thick slices of stale Italian bread, as coarse as
possible
300 ml (10 fl oz) milk
75 ml (3 fl oz) olive oil
1 clove garlic, crushed
5 canned tomatoes, chopped
a large pinch of oregano
salt and freshly milled pepper
450 g (16 oz) scamorza cheese (dried mozzarella)
or fresh mozzarella cheese

Place the bread on a plate and cover with the milk. When it is wet through, arrange the bread on the bottom of an ovenproof dish, making sure it is tightly packed together.

Fry the oil, garlic and tomatoes together in a saucepan for about 15 minutes. Season with the oregano, and salt and pepper to taste, then pour the tomato mixture over the bread. Arrange the sliced cheese on top. Bake in a preheated moderately hot oven (200°C, 400°F, gas mark 6) for about 15 minutes.

THE LUNCH TABLE (right) *Plates are superfluous with this wooden trough into which the pasta is piled; everyone around the table then simply helps themselves.*

26

CAPPUCCIO IMBOTTITO

Stuffed Cabbage Leaves

SERVES 6

2–3 tablespoons olive oil
1 large onion, chopped
400 g (14 oz) minced meat (beef, lamb, veal,
chicken etc.)
150 ml (5 fl oz) dry white wine
1 litre (1¾ pints) passata *(sieved tomatoes)*
about 12 large cabbage leaves
8 heaped tablespoons long-grain rice
freshly grated pecorino cheese, to taste
salt and freshly milled pepper

Heat the oil in a pan and fry the onion for about 6 minutes. Add the meat and brown it carefully all over. Add the wine and allow to evaporate for about 3 minutes, then add the *passata* and stir. Cover the pan and simmer the sauce for 20–30 minutes.

Meanwhile, bring a large pot of water to the boil and cook the cabbage leaves for 10–12 minutes or until they are just soft. Drain and leave to cool. Cook the rice in boiling salted water until just tender; drain.

Fill each cabbage leaf with about 1 tablespoonful of rice until all the rice is used up.

Pour some of the sauce over the bottom of an ovenproof dish and sprinkle the sauce with grated pecorino. Arrange the filled cabbage leaves on top and cover with the rest of the sauce and cheese. Bake in a preheated moderately hot oven (200°C, 400°F, gas mark 6) for about 15 minutes or until heated through. Serve hot or cold.

The dough for maltagliati (below) *which literally means 'badly cut', is made in the same way as any other pasta (see p. 136).*

When the dough has been rolled out, fold it into three and make rough, irregular cuts across it (bottom left). When all the dough has been cut, open out the strips and scatter them over a floured work top.

Leave the strips to dry out a little for about 10–20 minutes, then gather them together to use (below centre).

MALTAGLIATI AL SUGO DI POMODORO (below)

MALTAGLIATI AL SUGO DI POMODORO

Maltagliati with Tomato Sauce

SERVES 6

*5 tablespoons olive oil
1 onion, finely chopped
1 large stick celery, finely chopped
1 carrot, finely chopped
1 litre (1¾ pints)* passata *(sieved tomatoes)
salt and freshly milled pepper
600 g (1¼ lb)* maltagliati *or other pasta of your choice*
To finish
*a handful of fresh basil, rocket or coriander leaves,
torn into strips with your fingers
freshly grated Parmesan or pecorino cheese to taste*

Heat the oil in a saucepan and fry the onion, celery and carrot for about 3–5 minutes, then add the *passata* and season to taste. Simmer covered for about 30 minutes. Remove from the heat and allow the sauce to stand, covered, until required.

Bring a large pot of salted water to the boil. Toss in the pasta and cook until *al dente* (check packet for cooking time as brands vary). Drain the pasta and return to the pan. Pour the sauce over, toss together thoroughly and scatter the herb of your choice over the top. (I do not recommend a combination of these or any other herbs; choose one and stick to it.) Sprinkle generously with freshly grated Parmesan or pecorino and serve.

Maltagliati are left to dry out in the fresh air before use (right).

29

ROGNONE DI VITELLO ALLA FURNACELLA

Grilled Lamb's Kidneys

Although the original recipe uses kidneys, you can also prepare small lamb cutlets in this way.

SERVES *4–6*

1 kg (2¼ lb) lamb's kidneys
300 ml (10 fl oz) olive oil
150 ml (5 fl oz) white wine vinegar
a handful of fresh rosemary sprigs
salt and freshly milled pepper

Trim and rinse the kidneys carefully and cut them into neat slices. Mix the oil, vinegar and rosemary together in a shallow dish and lay the kidney slices in the mixture. Leave to marinate for at least 1 hour.

Remove the kidneys from the marinade and grill or barbecue for about 5–7 minutes on each side, brushing them with a branch of rosemary dipped in the remaining marinade as they cook. Sprinkle the kidneys with salt and pepper just before serving.

FARMHOUSE STORE *Baskets of freshly harvested citrus fruits are loaded into a cart, ready to be taken to market.*

ALBANESI

Albanian Biscuits

MAKES 20

1 wineglass of white wine
1 wineglass of olive oil
1 wineglass of caster sugar
plain flour – as required
granulated sugar for dusting
oil for greasing

Put the wine in a saucepan and add the oil. Bring to the boil, then add the sugar and stir until the sugar has dissolved. Stir in as much flour as the liquid will absorb, to make a smooth ball of dough rather like choux pastry. Tip it on to the work top and let it cool down.

Divide the dough into about 20 pieces and roll each one into a pencil shape with your hands, then roll it round into a ring shape. Dip the rings in granulated sugar and arrange on an oiled baking sheet. Bake in a preheated moderately hot oven (200°C, 400°F, gas mark 6) for about 12–15 minutes or until golden brown. Cool on a wire rack. Serve the biscuits with sparkling wine.

LA FESTA DI SAN GIUSEPPE

Giuseppe's Name Day

When virtually everyone in Italy was named after a saint, one's Name Day fell on the saint's day and the celebration would be almost the same as one's birthday. Nowadays, Italian children are baptized with a much wider variety of names of very different origins, so there are fewer Name Day celebrations than before.

San Giuseppe, or Saint Joseph, is one of Italy's most popular saints. I had looked forward very much to celebrating my friend Giuseppe's Name Day with him and his family on 19 March. He was one of the first people to teach me about cooking and has always, as long as I can remember, refused to eat pre-packaged food, long before any theory that preservatives and E numbers were perhaps not so wonderful after all. The olives with which we began his celebratory lunch, for instance, had been picked and bottled by Giuseppe himself to his own

recipe. Because he grows most of his own herbs and vegetables, everything he makes tastes incredibly fresh and delicious.

His minestrone is legendary and he always waxes lyrical about

how healthy it is because it's fat-free. Having been raised on it from the age of three months, I can certainly vouch for that.

He insisted on making his *fegato alla Veneziana*, although his wife

complained that she would have liked to do it for him. He let her make the mashed potatoes instead! I had the job of picking the tiny, first-of-the-season salad leaves which we ate with a perfect balsamic vinegar dressing. To finish off, Giulia, Giuseppe's mother-in-law, made him a wonderfully golden, eggy rice cake. There was only one thing left to do at this point, which was to aid the digestion of this wonderful meal with some of Giuseppe's own home-distilled grappa . . .

Menu

Olive Nere Marinate

Il Grande Minestrone Vegetale

Il Fegato alla Veneziana or *La Pizzaiola*

Insalatina all'Aceto Balsamico

Purè di Patate al Limone

Crostata di Marmellata or *La Torta di Riso di Giulia*

EARLY SPRING IN THE VENETO (left) *Weak rays of sunshine brighten a March day.*

NAME DAY CAKES (left) *One may well receive a special cake on one's Name Day – rather like a birthday.*

OLIVE NERE MARINATE

Marinated Black Olives

1 kg (2¼ lb) black olives
500 ml (18 fl oz) best quality olive oil
6 cloves garlic, crushed, then coarsely chopped
1 small red chilli pepper, finely chopped
a handful of fresh rosemary sprigs, leaves removed
and chopped
salt and freshly milled pepper

If the olives are fresh (i.e. picked off the tree) they must be soaked in cold water for 40 days, changing the water twice a day, in order to remove all the bitterness. If you are not using fresh olives, try to get olives preserved in brine; soak them in cold water overnight to remove the flavour of the brine. In both cases, rinse and dry the olives well once they have been appropriately soaked.

When the olives are ready, pack them into one or more large glass jars with tight-fitting lids. Mix the oil with all the other ingredients and pour it over the olives. The olives should be coated with oil but not swimming in it. Close the jars tightly and shake them to distribute the oil as evenly as possible. Keep in a cool place and use as required.

The olives improve with time but must be eaten within 3 months once opened. Serve as a delicious appetizer with wine and chunks of coarse bread to soak up the oil.

OLIVE NERE MARINATE

IL GRANDE MINESTRONE VEGETALE

Grand Vegetable Minestrone

SERVES 6

3 large carrots, diced
5–6 potatoes, peeled and diced
a handful of fresh spinach, chard or cabbage leaves, washed and shredded finely
2 large sticks celery, sliced
1 large onion, chopped
1 large clove garlic, chopped
a handful of fresh parsley, washed and chopped
about 1 litre (1¾ pt) water
salt and freshly milled pepper
2 vegetable stock cubes or 2 teaspoons vegetable extract
3 tablespoons tomato purée or 5 tablespoons chopped canned tomatoes
olive oil to taste
about 8 leaves of fresh basil, torn into pieces

Make sure all the vegetables are shredded finely or chopped neatly into very small cubes and place them, with the garlic and parsley, in a large pot. Add about 1 litre (1¾ pt) of cold water and add a pinch of salt, the stock cubes or vegetable extract and the tomato purée or chopped canned tomatoes. Cover and simmer gently for 1–2 hours, stirring occasionally.

When all the vegetables are soft and tender, remove from the heat. Just before serving, add olive oil and basil to taste – simply stir them into the soup without further cooking.

This soup can be served warm or cold but *never* hot. Parmesan cheese is superfluous.

Slice the onions very finely and rinse them thoroughly in cold water, before frying them with the sage leaves.

IL FEGATO ALLA VENEZIANA

Venetian Liver and Onions

SERVES 6–8

5 medium-sized onions, very finely sliced
3 walnut-sized knobs of butter
3 fresh sage leaves, rubbed
salt and freshly milled pepper
1 tablespoon vegetable oil
12 very thin, neat slices of calf's liver
purè di patate al limone (see below)

Rinse the onions thoroughly in cold water, then dry them with kitchen towel. Melt about 2 knobs of the butter in a wide pan with the sage and fry the onions until soft. Add salt and pepper to taste. Remove from the heat and set aside, but keep warm.

Melt the remaining butter in another wide pan with the oil and fry the liver very quickly, about 2–3 minutes each side. Season with salt and pepper and remove from the heat.

To serve, arrange the mashed potato on a platter, put the onions on top and the liver on top of them. Serve at once.

Fry the slices of liver very quickly. 2–3 minutes on each side is enough.

LA PIZZAIOLA

Beef Pizzaiola

SERVES 6

*6 very thin sirloin steaks, trimmed of all fat and
gristle
4 cloves garlic, finely chopped
4 tablespoons olive oil
400 g (14 oz) canned chopped tomatoes or passata
or a mixture of the two
½ heaped teaspoon dried oregano
½ heaped teaspoon pesto sauce or 1 tablespoon
chopped fresh basil
salt and freshly milled pepper*

You may need to use 2 frying pans or to make
this dish in 2 batches.

Pound the steaks until very thin with a meat
mallet. Heat the garlic and olive oil together in
a wide pan over a medium heat until the garlic
is golden brown. Add the tomatoes and bring
to the boil. Cook for about 5 minutes, stirring
the tomatoes frequently.

Stir in the oregano and pesto or basil, then
slide in the beef. Cook for a maximum of 2
minutes on each side, then remove from the
heat. Season to taste with salt and pepper and
transfer to a dish to serve.

This dish is excellent with mashed or boiled
potatoes and a green salad.

FRESH FROM THE GARDEN (right) *Tiny young
salad leaves from the first crop of the season are what
make this simple salad special.*

INSALATINA ALL' ACETO BALSAMICO

Tiny Salad Leaves with Balsamic Vinegar Dressing

SERVES 6–8

*4–5 handfuls of very young salad leaves including
lettuce, rocket, chicory, 'Little Gem' hearts etc.
1½ teaspoons balsamic vinegar
½ teaspoon salt
¼ teaspoon white pepper
6 tablespoons olive oil*

Wash and dry the salad leaves very carefully
and arrange in a bowl.

Mix the balsamic vinegar with the salt until
the salt is dissolved, then stir in the white
pepper and olive oil.

Taste the dressing to check it is correctly
seasoned for your taste, then pour on to the
salad. Toss everything together and serve.

PURÈ DI PATATE AL LIMONE

Mashed Potato with Lemon

SERVES 6–8

*6 large potatoes suitable for mashing
300 ml (½ pint) milk
300 ml (½ pint) water
salt and freshly milled pepper
30–55 g (2 oz) unsalted butter
grated rind of 1 very large lemon or 2 smaller ones*

Peel the potatoes and cut them into even-sized
pieces. Put them into a saucepan and cover
with the milk and the water. Add a large pinch
of salt. Bring to the boil and simmer them
gently until soft.

Drain off all excess liquid and mash carefully
with a fork, then push through a mouli to
make a really smooth purée. Stir in the butter,
the lemon rind and pepper to taste. Serve at
once, or reheat briefly just before serving.

TILED KITCHEN (right) *Still lifes and kitchen
implements combine the aesthetic and the practical in
a typically Italian way.*

CROSTATA DI MARMELLATA

Plum Jam and Amaretto Tart

MAKES ONE 30 CM (12 IN) TART

Pastry
500 g (1 lb 2 oz) plain flour
150 g (5 oz) caster sugar
325 g (11½ oz) butter
3 egg yolks
a pinch of salt
butter for greasing

Filling
a 500 g (1 lb 2 oz) jar sour plum or sour cherry jam
6–8 amaretti biscuits, broken up
1 heaped tablespoon unsweetened cocoa
icing sugar for dusting

Sift the flour on to the work top in a pile and make a hole in the centre; put the sugar and butter into this hole with the egg yolks and salt. Blend everything together quickly with your fingertips (do not knead). When it is an amalgamated ball, put in a plastic bag and rest in the refrigerator for about 30 minutes.

Mix the jam, crushed biscuits and cocoa together until smooth. Roll the pastry out fairly thick. Use to line a buttered 30 cm (12 in) loose-bottomed flan tin. Press down around the edges to create a crust. Spoon the jam filling into the centre and smooth it out. Roll out the pastry trimmings and cut into rounds. Arrange on top of the filling.

Bake in a preheated moderate oven (200°C, 400°F, gas mark 6) for 20 minutes, then turn down to 180°C, 350°F, gas mark 4, and bake for a further 20–25 minutes, or until golden brown. Remove from the oven and cool. Dust with icing sugar before serving.

LA TORTA DI RISO DI GIULIA

Giulia's Rice Cake

MAKES ONE 25 CM (10 IN) CAKE

150 g (5 oz) short-grain rice
1.1 litres (38 fl oz) milk
butter for greasing
2 tablespoons semolina
8 eggs
400 g (14 oz) caster sugar
3 tablespoons brandy
juice of ½ lemon or grated rind of ½ lemon

Put the rice and 600 ml (1 pint) of the milk in a saucepan and bring to the boil. Cook for 10 minutes, then drain.

Butter a 25 cm (10 in) cake tin thoroughly and scatter the semolina over the butter. Do not use a loose-bottomed tin or the liquid will ooze out. Turn the cake tin upside down to remove any loose semolina.

Beat the eggs in a large bowl until foaming and pale yellow. Add the sugar a little at a time, beating constantly, followed by the brandy and the lemon juice or rind. Stir very thoroughly before adding the rice and the remaining 500 ml (18 fl oz) milk. Pour the mixture into the cake tin.

Bake in the centre of a preheated moderate oven (180°C, 350°F, gas mark 4) for about 50 minutes or until a wooden cocktail stick inserted into the centre comes out clean. The cake should be set and golden brown. Serve warm or cold.

KITCHEN UTENSILS (left)

LA TORTA DI RISO DI GIULIA (right)

Butter the cake tin thoroughly before scattering in the semolina.

Stir the egg mixture well before adding the rice and remaining milk.

UN PICNIC LUNIGIANO

Tuscan Picnic

Although I was born and educated in Rome, my summers were spent in Tuscany where my parents and other branches of the family had villas. The family estates encompassed sprawling vineyards and silver-grey olive groves, which in my mother's time yielded olives which at harvest time were pressed to make the estate's own oil. It is from this landscape of rolling, umber-coloured hills, endless vineyards and intense blue seas that my happiest and most vivid memories come. In returning to Tuscany I slip back instantly into this land and its way of life with the very deepest sense of having come home.

One day in May I decided to take my own children back to one of the picnic haunts of my childhood. Picnicking is something Italians do a lot. Weather permitting, on *Pasquetta*, Easter Monday, the entire family including grandmama, newborn baby and all, set off for the countryside for the annual *scampagnata*, or outing. And during the summer months many families take to the cool of the shady hills and hold their picnics there, often lighting dan-

gerous fires on which they cook their pasta. These cooking fires can be a problem if not built safely and the buzz of summer insects is often drowned by the buzz of mountain patrol helicopters during these months.

When I was a child, my parents used to organize picnics for me and my brothers as often as possible during the warm days. We would always choose a site that was near cool running water and in a place where we were allowed to light a safe fire, so that we could enjoy one of the real picnic treats – freshly cooked pasta – in the open air.

On the day I took my own children off for a picnic, the spot I chose was down by the river and to get there we had to park the cars some way off and then wind our way through the long grass and poppies all the way to the river bank. We found a narrow

THE PASTA POT *Spaghetti cooked out of doors on an open fire and served with even the simplest sauce or dressing always tastes surprisingly good.*

strip of land covered in cool, soft green grass that jutted out into the river and a nearby wooden jetty which was perfect for laying out the food. As we had quite a lot to carry, the walk was arduous enough to make getting there worthwhile and cool dips in the river were definitely the first item on the agenda.

The next task was to select some flat white stones to make a secure circle for the fire. We then built our fire in the centre, using all the odd bits of driftwood we could find. Once we had glowing red embers, the grill was laid on top and the water could then be boiled for our pasta.

Eating pasta which has been cooked out of doors under a summer sky is one of the most delicious experiences. All you need is a pot, enough fresh, clean water in which to cook the spaghetti and some salt. I chose a very simple oil and garlic dressing for this picnic, but you can take along a ready-made sauce of any kind you prefer.

As well as the menu listed here, I also took plenty of bread and Parma ham, salame, Parmesan cheese in chunks, firm red toma-

YOUNG ROMANS *Voluminous towels and a bush of wild sage growing nearby provided the props for this impromptu re-enactment of the Roman Empire.*

toes and fresh fruit. Many Italian foods seem almost made for picnics with the wealth of different cold meats and cheeses, breads like focaccia, which can be split open to make envelopes into which any number of fillings can be stuffed, and the quality of fresh vegetables and fruit which need no further preparation. Having said that, preparing some simple dishes at home or packing the ingredients to combine at the picnic spot adds a far more special touch to the occasion and all the food I prepared and took along for this picnic was ideal for hearty, outdoor appetites. Fresh fruit provided a suitably refreshing conclusion to the meal – pear slices dipped into creamy mascarpone cheese and luxurious soft peaches soaked in lots of red wine.

After lunch, my sons dressed up as Roman Emperors with crowns of wild sage around their heads and then we waded downstream on an exploration trip. On the river bank the boys soon discovered a hunter's shelter made out of green boughs and we nestled inside, with me telling them stories of the picnics of my own childhood – until they got hungry again and we all had to go and eat up the rest of the picnic.

Menu

Spaghetti Aglio e Olio

Mozzarella con Verdura Mista

Frittata di Cipolla

Insalata di Pollo

Pane, Fichi e Alici

Pesche al Vino

Mascarpone con le Pere

SPAGHETTI AGLIO E OLIO

Spaghetti with Oil and Garlic

SERVES 6

500 g (1 lb 2 oz) fine spaghetti or spaghettini
salt and freshly milled pepper
2–5 cloves garlic, crushed
about 200 ml (7 fl oz) olive oil
1 dried red chilli pepper (optional)

First light the fire. Let the flames die down and then make sure you have a good constant base of hot embers and low flames which are required for boiling water. If the fire is surrounded by stones, you can lay the grill over the fire so that it rests flat on the stones; put the pot of salted water on the top. Put a lid on the pot and bring the water to the boil. Toss in the spaghetti, stir to prevent sticking and cook until *al dente*.

Meanwhile, put the garlic and oil into a small pan and heat them together over the fire, next to the boiling pot of spaghetti. The garlic should go really dark brown and crispy. If you want to, you can put the chilli pepper in with the garlic as well.

When the garlic is blackened, throw it away (the same applies to the chilli). By now, the spaghetti must be ready to drain. Holding the lid on firmly, tip the pot over and pour out the water, but not the spaghetti (alternatively, pack a colander). Try to drain the pasta fairly well. Pour the flavoured oil into the pot and toss with the spaghetti using 2 forks. (If you have not used the chilli, season with freshly milled black pepper.) Serve at once.

MOZZARELLA CON VERDURA MISTA

Mozzarella with Mixed Vegetables

SERVES 6

12 slices of marmande tomato
12 slices of mozzarella cheese (same size as the tomato)
200 g (7 oz) mixed vegetables, finely chopped, to include spring onions, peppers, courgettes, carrots and cucumbers
75 g (2½ oz) capers, rinsed and dried carefully
about 8 tablespoons olive oil
salt and freshly milled pepper

Arrange the tomato slices on a wide platter or in boxes and cover with the mozzarella slices. Cover each one with a little of the chopped mixed vegetables. Arrange the capers on top, then douse each one with olive oil and sprinkle with salt and pepper. Cover tightly to take on the picnic. Alternatively, take all the ingredients prepared in advance and put them all together at the last minute.

FRITTATA DI CIPOLLA

Flat Onion Omelette

This is one to make at home and take with you to eat cold.

SERVES 6

10 eggs, beaten
salt and freshly milled pepper
3 large onions, thinly sliced
8 tablespoons olive oil

Beat the eggs very thoroughly with plenty of salt and pepper. Rinse and dry the sliced onions thoroughly. Heat half the olive oil in a large frying pan and fry the onions until soft, stirring occasionally, without allowing them to brown. Cool the cooked onions and season with a little salt. Tip the cooked, cold onions into the egg mixture.

Wipe the frying pan completely clean and pour the remaining oil into it. Heat the oil until smoking hot, then tip the egg and onion mixture into the pan. Fry on one side for 3–5 minutes or until browned and fairly firm. Place a large lid or plate on the pan and turn the omelette out on to the lid or plate, so that it comes out upside down. Slide it back into the pan the other way up so that the uncooked side can brown and firm. Turn it out again in the same way, cool and serve cut in wedges.

MOZZARELLA CON VERDURA MISTA (left),
FRITTATA DI CIPOLLA (right)

INSALATA DI POLLO

Chicken Salad

*To prevent the salad leaves from becoming soggy,
take the washed and dried endive with you in one
container and the marinating chicken in another.
You can then put the two together at the last minute
on a wide plastic tray.*

SERVES 6

50 g (1¾ oz) sultanas
3–4 skinned chicken breasts, boiled
2 teaspoons grated lemon rind
5 tablespoons oil
juice of 2 lemons
3 tablespoons chopped fresh parsley
salt
1 head curly endive

Soak the sultanas in cold water for about 20 minutes. Slice the chicken breasts thinly and put them in a bowl. Mix the oil and lemon juice together, then add the parsley, lemon rind and salt to taste. Cover the chicken breasts with this marinade.

Drain the sultanas, scatter them over the chicken and mix everything together. Cover and marinate until required, then serve on a bed of curly endive.

PANE, FICHI E ALICI

Bread, Figs and Anchovies

Take the whole loaf of bread and cut it at the picnic, but prepare the rest of the ingredients beforehand and take them packed in boxes.

SERVES 6

6–8 fillets of salted or canned anchovies, rinsed thoroughly
600 g (1¼ lb) fresh, ripe figs, peeled
2 cloves garlic, very finely chopped
6 thick slices of bread
about 6 tablespoons olive oil
4 spring onions, finely chopped

Make sure all of the salt has been washed off the anchovies, then remove any remaining bones. If using canned anchovies, rinse them thoroughly to remove all the oil. Mash the anchovies and figs together (alternatively, whizz in the food processor). Add the garlic.

Sprinkle the slices of bread with oil, spread with the fig mixture and scatter the spring onion on top. Any remaining oil can be drizzled over the onion.

PESCE AL VINO (above), MASCARPONE CON LE PERE (below)

PESCHE AL VINO

Peaches in Red Wine

You can either let everybody do their own or prepare a bowl of peaches in advance.
Other fruit such as pears and apricots are also good served this way.

SERVES 6

6–12 peaches (depending on how large they are)
about 500 ml (18 fl oz) dry red or white wine
sugar to taste (optional)

Slice the unpeeled peaches into the red wine. Sprinkle with a little sugar if desired and leave to macerate for as long as you like.

Eat the peaches first, then drink the wonderfully flavoured wine – then lie back and fall asleep in the shade!

MASCARPONE CON LE PERE

Mascarpone with Pears

SERVES 6

6 ripe, firm pears
about 300 g (11 oz) mascarpone cheese

Peel the pears and slice into easily holdable pieces. Dip and scoop into the mascarpone as your fancy takes you, or spread each piece of pear thickly with the cheese and arrange them all on a platter.

A PRANZO DA ELEONORA

Dinner with Eleonora

Sicily's best known and most respected cookery expert is my dear friend Eleonora Consoli. I first met Eleonora through the Count and Countess Notabartolo on their estate at Lentini, when we spent time there filming for my cookery series for BBC television, and we have been friends ever since. I simply cannot visit the island without seeing her and my last visit was no exception.

As usual, Eleonora was organizing some kind of get-together and invited me along. It turned out to be a girls' night, in honour of the *Festa della Donna*, the day when all of Italy celebrates women. It seemed slightly out of place to be celebrating this in Sicily, where many advances which women elsewhere take for granted still present an uphill struggle, but I was happy just to be in Eleonora's company again.

APERITIFS BEFORE DINNER (right)
Dinner with Eleonora Consoli, who presents her own cookery programme on Italy's RAI channel, guarantees not only delicious, but also extremely interesting food.

It is a wonderful thing to discover in another cook the same passion and drive about food that I feel. Eleonora has taught me so much about the food of Sicily and its myriad traditions and her love for her island and its cuisine is absolutely infectious. Because she knows how I want to enlarge my repertoire of Sicilian cooking, on this evening she prepared dishes with which I was not familiar. We began with the *timballo del Gattopardo*, the Leopard's timbale – an allusion to the prince of that name in Lampedusa's novel *The Leopard*, which evokes the enchanting lost world of the Sicilian nobility of the last century. It is a typical baroque dish, so characteristic of Sicily in being gloriously complicated and rich.

Menu

Il Timballo del Gattopardo

Nasello al Gratin

Nidi di Scuma

Falsomagro al Sugo

Gelo di Cannella

Eleonora then prepared a delicious baby cod. Because nothing in Sicilian cuisine is ever really simple – though it may deceive you into thinking that it is – surrounding the fish were deep-fried nests of pasta filled with fresh peas. The quintessential Sicilian meat dish followed – *il falso-magro*, literally 'fake lean'.

When Eleonora brought out the dessert she smiled at me – she knows just how much I adore this delightfully refreshing cinnamon-flavoured jelly. As she sat down she whispered quietly to me, 'It was the Leopard's favourite dessert, too!'

IL TIMBALLO DEL GATTOPARDO
Enjoyed against the superb backdrop of Palermo, the dinner evoked the magical world of Lampedusa's Sicily.

IL TIMBALLO DEL GATTOPARDO

The Leopard's Timbale

SERVES 8

Pastry

500 g (1 lb 2 oz) plain flour
250 g (9 oz) unsalted butter
120 g (4 oz) sugar
3 eggs
a pinch of salt
1 teaspoon grated lemon rind

Filling

9 tablespoons olive oil
2 onions, chopped
200 g (7 oz) shelled fresh peas or frozen petit pois
250 g (9 oz) rump steak, trimmed and chopped coarsely
330 ml (11 fl oz) beef stock
200 g (7 oz) chicken livers
1 clove
salt and freshly milled pepper
300 g (11 oz) short macaroni
2 hard-boiled eggs, shelled and chopped
5–6 tablespoons ricotta or other fresh soft cheese
300 g (11 oz) cooked ham, chopped
8 tablespoons freshly grated Parmesan cheese
2 egg yolks, beaten

To make the pastry, sift the flour on to the work top in a pile and plunge your fist into the centre to make a hole; put the butter and sugar into this hole with the eggs, salt and grated lemon rind. Blend all these ingredients together quickly with your fingertips to make a smooth ball of dough. Be careful not to knead it too much or it will become heavy. Put the dough in a bowl, cover with a cloth and chill until required.

For the filling, heat half the olive oil in a saucepan and fry one of the onions with the peas until soft. Add the meat. Cover and simmer gently for about 20 minutes, adding the stock gradually.

Meanwhile, fry the other onion in the remaining olive oil in a frying pan for about 5 minutes. Add the chicken livers and the clove and cook everything briefly until the chicken livers have become slightly crumbly. Season with salt and pepper to taste. Remove from the heat and set aside.

Bring a large pot of salted water to the boil and cook the macaroni until *al dente* (check packet for cooking time as brands vary). Drain the pasta and dress it with the juices from the meat and pea sauce.

Roll out two-thirds of the dough to a thickness of about 5 mm (¼ in) and use to line a greased 25 cm (10 in) pie or cake tin. Put a layer of macaroni on the bottom, then cover with alternating layers of peas and rump steak, chicken livers, hard-boiled egg, ricotta and chopped ham. Continue to layer until you fill the pastry case, sprinkling the layers from time to time with grated Parmesan.

Roll out the remaining dough and cut out a round to fit the top of the tin. Lay the dough over the filling, and pinch the edges together securely to seal. Brush with the beaten egg yolks and pierce the top in several places to let the steam escape.

Bake in a preheated moderately hot oven (190°C, 375°F, gas mark 5) for about 1 hour or until golden brown.

Let the timbale stand in its tin for about 10–15 minutes after it comes out of the oven: the pie crust will then pull away from the side of the tin, making it easier to serve. Serve directly from the tin or turn the timbale carefully out on to a platter.

NASELLO AL GRATIN

Baked Baby Cod

SERVES 6

1 whole baby cod or other white fish such as whiting, weighing about 1 kg (2 ¼ lb), gutted
120 g (4 oz) fresh breadcrumbs
8 tablespoons chopped fresh parsley
salt and freshly milled pepper
5 tablespoons olive oil
50 g (1¾ oz) can anchovies, drained
juice of 2 lemons

Open the fish out flat as much as possible, placing it on its back in a baking dish. Cover the fish with about half the breadcrumbs, half the parsley and salt and pepper to taste. Heat the oil in a small pan and add the anchovies, mashing them in the hot oil to make a smooth sauce. (Alternatively, blend the anchovies and oil in a food processor.) Pour this all over the fish and cover with the remaining bread-crumbs and parsley.

Bake in a preheated moderate oven (180°C, 350°F, gas mark 4) for 30–40 minutes or until the fish will flake easily when tested with a fork. Sprinkle over the lemon juice and serve.

NIDI DI SCUMA

Fried Pasta Nests

SERVES 4–6

225 g (8 oz) fine capellini pasta nests
salt
oil for deep frying
cooked vegetables, such as peas, onions
or mushrooms

Bring a large pot of salted water to the boil. Toss in the pasta nests and cook until *al dente* (check packet for cooking time as brands vary). Drain and allow to cool until just tepid.

Heat a large pan of oil until a small piece of bread dropped into it sizzles instantly. Re-shape the cooked noodles into nest shapes, by twisting them around a fork. Using a slotted spoon, lower them into the hot oil, one or two at a time. Let them fry until crisp and golden, then remove with a slotted spoon and drain on kitchen paper to remove excess oil.

Fill these nests with freshly cooked vegetables of your choice, such as braised peas and onions, braised mushrooms or artichokes, stewed courgettes or peppers. Serve hot.

FILLING THE PASTA NESTS *Any cooked vegetables – on this occasion we had braised peas – can be used to fill the pasta nests.*

FALSOMAGRO
AL SUGO

Sicilian Stuffed Meat Roll

SERVES 6

700 g (1½ lb) boneless veal in one large, thick slice
300 g (11 oz) minced veal
75 g (2½ oz) fresh breadcrumbs
75 g (2½ oz) caciocavallo or Parmesan cheese,
freshly grated
2 hard-boiled eggs, shelled and chopped
1 egg
salt and freshly milled pepper
freshly grated nutmeg or ground cinnamon
50 g (2 oz) tuma, provola or provolone cheese,
sliced
50 g (1¾ oz) mortadella or salame
4–6 tablespoons olive oil
1 onion, chopped
1 carrot, chopped
1 stick celery, chopped
2 heaped tablespoons tomato purée
400 g (14 oz) can tomatoes
1 clove
150 ml (5 fl oz) dry red wine

Using a meat mallet, flatten the slice of veal as much as possible to make one large, very thin sheet of meat. If necessary use more than one slice and overlap them as you use the mallet to create a similar effect. Place the sheet of meat on a wet cloth or tea towel.

Mix the minced veal thoroughly with the breadcrumbs and caciocavallo or Parmesan. Add to this mixture the two chopped hard-boiled eggs and the raw egg to bind the stuffing together. Season with salt, pepper and nutmeg or cinnamon.

Before the ingredients are piled up on top, it is important that the veal used for falsomagro *has been flattened until it is as thin as possible; otherwise the roll will be too thick.*

FALSOMAGRO, *served with a tomato sauce. This stuffed meat roll, which is equally delicious served hot or cold, is a typically Sicilian dish in its richness and elaborateness.*

Spread the stuffing over the meat, leaving a border around the edges. Cover the stuffing with the slices of tuma, provola or provolone and then with the slices of mortadella or salame. Roll the meat up lengthways like a Swiss roll, using the wet cloth or tea towel to help and drawing the ends together very tightly in order to squeeze the roll closed. Remove the cloth and tie the roll securely with kitchen string.

Heat the olive oil in a wide saucepan and fry the chopped onion, carrot and celery until the onion is soft and translucent. Moisten with a little water every now and again. (Instead of water you could use the juice from the canned tomatoes.) Stir in the tomato purée. Cook for about 10 minutes, then add the drained, chopped tomatoes and clove. Season with salt, pepper and nutmeg or cinnamon and continue to simmer gently for about 15 minutes.

Lay the meat roll in the pan and spoon the sauce all over it – as though you were basting the meat. Pour in the red wine and allow the fumes to evaporate, then add enough water just to cover the meat. Cover the pan and simmer very gently for about 1½ hours. Check the pan occasionally and if necessary add more water to the meat as it simmers.

To serve, remove the meat roll from the pan and take off the string. Slice the meat thinly and arrange it on a platter. Reduce the sauce in the pan over a lively heat, until it has reduced by about half, then pour it all over the sliced meat. Serve hot or cold.

GELO DI CANNELLA

Cinnamon Jelly

SERVES 6

10 g (⅓ oz) cinnamon sticks
800 ml (1⅓ pints) cold water
300 g (11 oz) caster sugar
65 g (2¼ oz) cornflour
50 g (1¾ oz) chocolat pâtissier, *finely chopped*
(optional)
lemon leaves, to decorate

Put the cinnamon sticks and cold water into a saucepan. Place over a medium heat and bring to the boil, then boil gently for about 5 minutes. Remove from the heat and leave to stand for 12 hours.

Strain the cinnamon liquid carefully and return to the pan. Add the sugar. Dissolve the cornflour in 2 tablespoons of the cinnamon liquid and add to the rest of the ingredients in the pan. Bring to the boil, stirring constantly, and boil very gently until thickened. Remove from the heat and add the chocolate if using. Stir until the chocolate has melted.

Turn into one large or 6 small individual moulds and chill until solid. Turn out to serve, decorated with lemon leaves.

GELO DI CANNELLA (left), *decorated with strawberries, cherries and apricots.*

IN THE KITCHEN (far left) *Eleonora (in the foreground) had us all involved in the preparations.*

LA BISTECCATA

A Barbecue in Ronchi

If you are lucky enough to have your barbecue in a beautiful setting, and have access to plenty of scented, pungent wood which will lend wonderful flavours to your food, then I think you are on the way to having the most delicious of all meals. Food always tastes better out of doors in any case, and the effort of lighting the fire, cutting the wood into a suitable size and tending the fire and the food throughout the whole operation does wonders for the appetite.

All over Italy tremendous importance is placed on the wood used to make the fire. In Sicily, for example, they like to use lemon wood because it gives the food a unique citrus flavour. In Alto Adige, larch is used to cook polenta because it gives the finished dish such a deliciously smoky taste. At home in Tuscany we always use pine cones to get the fire going, and then use a combination of pine and apple wood for the actual cooking. I often throw some herbs on the fire, too, to add a special flavour to the food – fresh rosemary is wonderful with lamb and dried bay leaves really add to beef.

The disadvantage – and advantage – with our barbecue is that it is a permanent construction of stone, wood and cement with an extremely deep hole in the top where the fire is built. This means that the fire really does have to be enormous, so it's never worth having a barbecue unless we are cooking huge amounts of food! If we are having a barbecue at lunchtime for example, we really need to have the fire lit by about ten o'clock in the morning.

If it is at all possible, even if you are only using charcoal, have more than one fire going, with separate grills – or a very wide fire with more than one grill, so that you can cook lots of different things without the flavours becoming mixed up. In this menu, you could put all the meat on to one grill and cook the mussel kebabs on a different grill over the same fire. (You could also cook the kebabs on one of those grills specially made for cooking small fish, which save them from dropping straight into the burning embers. This is not essential, but it will make life a lot easier.) When I cook a barbecue with so many different foods and flavours, I usually ask someone to bring their portable barbecue along to ease matters.

The best thing about a barbecue is that there will always be plenty of joining in. The more people who become involved, the more fun the event will be – and the less work there will be for the cook. It is quite strange how even the most kitchen-shy man will become a fully qualified chef once he's within feet of the barbecue. Maybe it's something to do with age-old instincts and mammoth hunting, but I think that if a man (or a group of men) wants to take care of the cooking at a barbecue, then he should be encouraged to do so!

The best piece of advice I was ever given regarding the success of a barbecue is this – make sure the table at which everyone is eating is a good long way from the fire. Although you'll have further to walk back and forth with the food, you won't risk smoking anybody out and you give the cook – or cooks – plenty of space.

Menu

Spiedini di Cozze

Hamburger all'Italiana

Hamburger Piccanti

Abbacchio a Scottadito

Spiedini d'Agnello con Peperone

Spiedini di Manzo

Radicchio ai Ferri

Peperoni ai Ferri

Bruschetta

Banane al Cioccolato

GRILLING HAMBURGERS (left) *If you are fortunate enough to have such a large barbecue you can cook food with very different flavours.*

SPIEDINI D'AGNELLO CON PEPERONE (left)

SPIEDINI DI COZZE

Mussel Kebabs

SERVES 6

6 dozen mussels
250 g (8½ oz) streaky bacon, sliced as thinly as
possible, rind removed
4 cloves garlic, finely chopped
5 tablespoons very finely chopped fresh parsley
salt and freshly milled pepper
2 eggs, beaten
12–16 tablespoons fresh breadcrumbs

Scrub and clean the mussels thoroughly, being
sure to remove the beard. Place them all in a
wide pan and put over a lively heat with the lid
on. Give them about 5 minutes to open up,
shaking the pan occasionally to help them
open, then remove from the heat. Discard any
mussels that have not opened and remove the
others from their shells.

Cut the rashers of bacon into squares of
about the same size as the mussels. Arrange
the mussels and bacon squares alternately on
kebab skewers.

Mix the garlic and parsley together with the
breadcrumbs and add a little salt and pepper.
Roll the kebabs in the beaten egg then in the
breadcrumb mixture. Grill them on the barbecue over a gentle heat for about 3 minutes on
each side or until crisp. Serve hot.

STEAMED MUSSELS *A barbecue does not have to*
consist of all meat.

HAMBURGER ALL'ITALIANA

Italian Hamburgers

SERVES 6

1 kg (2¼ lb) lean minced beef
150 g (5 oz) stoned green olives, sliced or chopped
1 onion, chopped
1 egg
salt and freshly milled pepper
3 tablespoons olive oil

Mix together the beef, olives, onion, egg and salt and pepper to taste. Shape into 6 flat, thick discs. Brush with olive oil on both sides.

Grill on the barbecue over a medium heat for about 4 minutes on each side.

HAMBURGER PICCANTI

Hamburgers with Chilli

SERVES 6

1 kg (2¼ lb) lean minced beef
3 eggs
a large pinch of chilli powder (or more to taste)
2 tablespoons capers, rinsed and chopped
a pinch of dried mint
2–3 tablespoons freshly grated Parmesan cheese
salt
3 tablespoons olive oil

Mix the minced beef with the eggs, chilli powder, capers, mint, cheese and salt to taste. Shape into 6 flat, thick discs and brush them on both sides with oil.

Grill on the barbecue over a medium heat for about 4 minutes on each side.

Serve with a crisp salad or with lots of fresh crusty bread.

SPIEDINI DI COZZE (left)

FRESH ROSEMARY (right) *Throw some fresh rosemary on to the fire as the lamb cooks; it will give it a very special flavour.*

ABBACHIO A SCOTTADITO

'Burn your Fingers' Lamb Cutlets

SERVES 6

12 small lamb cutlets
2 cloves garlic
salt and freshly milled pepper
4 tablespoons olive oil

Rub the cutlets all over with the peeled garlic and sprinkle generously with salt and freshly milled pepper.

Grill on the barbecue over a medium heat for 3–4 minutes on each side, brushing liberally with olive oil as they cook.

SPIEDINI D'AGNELLO CON PEPERONE

Lamb Kebabs with Green Peppers

SERVES 6–8

1 kg (2¼ lb) boned shoulder of lamb
2 green peppers

salt and freshly milled pepper
branches of fresh rosemary
1 wineglass of olive oil

Cut the meat into quite wide and thick chunks – about 4 cm (1¾ in) wide and at least 3 cm (1¼ in) thick. Cut the peppers in half, remove the seeds and the membranes and cut into equal-sized pieces. Thread the meat and the peppers alternately on to kebab sticks or sticks of scented wood such as rosemary or bay which you can whittle especially for this dish. Make sure you pack everything very tightly on to the sticks. Season generously with salt and pepper.

Grill on the barbecue over a medium heat for about 6 minutes on each side. While the kebabs cook, dip the branches of rosemary into the olive oil and brush over the meat frequently. Serve very hot.

SPIEDINI D'AGNELLO CON PEPERONE

SPIEDINI DI MANZO

Beef Kebabs

Throw some dried bay leaves on to the fire to impart a special flavour to the meat.

SERVES 6

1 yellow pepper
1 kg (2¼ lb) lean beef steak, cut into even-sized chunks
2 onions, cut into quarters
about 18 mushrooms preserved in olive oil, or button mushrooms
about 20 black olives, stoned
about 12 bay leaves
salt and freshly milled pepper
4 tablespoons olive oil

Bring a pan of water to the boil, toss in the pepper and blanch for about 3 minutes. Drain, then cut the pepper into strips, removing all the seeds and membrane.

Alternate the chunks of beef on kebab skewers with pieces of onion, mushrooms, slices of yellow pepper, olives and bay leaves. Sprinkle with salt and pepper, then baste generously with oil.

Grill on the barbecue over a medium to high heat for about 4 minutes on each side.

RADICCHIO AI FERRI (right) *Other vegetables such as aubergines and fennel can be coated with oil and grilled in this way too.*

RADICCHIO AI FERRI

Grilled Radicchio

SERVES 6

3 large firm heads of radicchio, with as much root or base as possible
9 tablespoons olive oil
salt
freshly milled pepper

Cut the heads of radicchio in half and wash all 6 pieces carefully. Shake them dry, holding them by the base. Mix the olive oil and salt and pepper together and immerse the radicchio in the oil; be sure they are well coated.

Grill the radicchio on the barbecue over a medium heat for about 4 minutes on each side, pressing down firmly to flatten them as much as possible.

Make sure the metal of the grill is thoroughly hot before you begin to cook, otherwise the radicchio will fall apart.

59

PEPERONI AI FERRI

Grilled Peppers

SERVES 6

4 large, fleshy peppers, any colour
salt
6–8 tablespoons olive oil
3 cloves garlic, finely chopped
3 tablespoons chopped fresh parsley
freshly milled black pepper

Bring a large pot of salted water to the boil and toss in the whole peppers. Blanch for about 2 minutes, then drain them. Cut them in half lengthways, and remove all the seeds and membranes. Cut them in half again and brush all over with a little oil.

Grill them on the barbecue over medium heat for about 2 minutes on each side or until just softened. Transfer them to a dish and sprinkle with the garlic, parsley, black pepper to taste and remaining oil. Allow to marinate for about 15 minutes before serving.

PEPERONI AI FERRI (left)

TENDING THE BARBECUE *The barbecue in my garden is so deep it takes hours to get the fire going, so it's only worth it if I cook huge amounts of food – the perfect excuse.*

BRUSCHETTA

Italian Barbecued Toast

SERVES 6

12 thick slices of pane ciabatta
2 cloves garlic
7 tablespoons olive oil
salt and freshly milled pepper

Toast the bread on both sides on the barbecue over a medium heat, then remove from the grill and rub generously all over with the peeled garlic. Drench with olive oil, sprinkle with salt and pepper and serve quickly whilst it is still crisp and warm.

BANANE AL CIOCCOLATO

Chocolate Bananas

SERVES 6

6 large, firm bananas
175–200 g (6–7 oz) high quality plain, bitter
chocolate, chopped roughly

Slice open the bananas lengthways without peeling them and without cutting them completely in half. Insert the chocolate along each slit. Close the peel around the bananas and wrap each one tightly in foil. Grill on the barbecue over a medium to low heat, turning them over halfway through cooking, for about 6–8 minutes or until the bananas are soft and the chocolate runny. Serve with lots of soft Italian vanilla ice cream.

UNA COLAZIONE MILANESE

Chic Milanese Lunch

It doesn't seem to matter what I wear in Milan, I still feel utterly dowdy and completely under-dressed for any occasion. The lunch my cousin Gianluca gave at his flat was no exception.

Being young and rich in Milan means having an elegant address, lots of equally elegant friends and lots of money to spend on the good things in life. Milan has the best known *nouvelle cuisine* restaurant in Italy, owned and created by Gualtiero Marchesi. To my mind, this is the only Italian city in which such a restaurant could actually survive. The city has an extraordinary flair which I have never come across elsewhere in Italy, and only very rarely elsewhere in the world, and much of its considerable wealth seems to be happily spent on simply enjoying life.

Gianluca's lunch was typical of this philosophy. The food was beautifully presented and the company was beautifully but

GIANLUCA'S KITCHEN (right) *The antique, marble-topped dining table is the centrepiece of this elegant kitchen.*

unpretentiously dressed. In the elegant kitchen, with its antique central table, we began with a delicious combination of bright yellow Milanese risotto rice with asparagus. To follow, there were perfect deep-fried courgette flowers and thin pancakes filled with a delightful mixture of spinach and ricotta. The crispy mozzarella *in carrozza*, literally 'in a carriage', had been sandwiched in white bread and deep fried. Finally, there were fresh figs, beautifully arranged on top of a light zabaglione, to finish off the meal in a suitably stylish Milanese way.

Menu

Asparagi alla Milanese

Fiori di Zucchine

Crespelle di Ricotta e Spinaci

Mozzarella in Carrozza

Fichi Verdi con Zabaglione di Prosecco

LUNCH WITH FRIENDS (right) *Wealthy Milan puts a high priority on enjoying the good things in life.*

ASPARAGI ALLA MILANESE

Milanese Asparagus

SERVES 6

100 g (3½ oz) butter
1 small onion, finely chopped
600 g (1¼ lb) risotto rice
200 ml (7 fl oz) dry white wine
salt and freshly milled pepper
2 litres (3½ pints) vegetable or chicken stock,
kept hot
30 asparagus spears, trimmed
2 sachets saffron powder, or a large pinch of saffron
threads steeped in 4 tablespoons hot water
50 g (1 ¾ oz) Parmesan cheese, freshly grated
6 eggs

Melt half the butter in a heavy-bottomed saucepan and fry the onion until soft. Add the rice and stir to coat it with butter and onion. Add the wine and cook, stirring, until you can no longer smell the fumes from the alcohol.

Begin to add the stock, one ladleful at a time, stirring constantly to prevent sticking and to distribute the flavouring and the liquid equally. Never add more liquid until the previous quantity has been absorbed into the risotto. The risotto will take about 20 minutes to make from the moment that you add the rice to the onion.

FRESH ASPARAGUS (left) *Lombardy is noted for its excellent asparagus which grows in many areas around Milan.*

Whilst the risotto is cooking, steam the asparagus until tender (about 11 minutes).

5 minutes before the risotto is finished, add the saffron powder or liquid and stir it in very thoroughly. Season to taste with salt and pepper. As soon as the rice is tender and properly swollen, add half the remaining butter and the Parmesan. Remove from the heat, cover and let it stand for 2–3 minutes.

Meanwhile, heat the remaining butter in a big frying pan and fry the six eggs until just set. (You may like to use more butter or oil.)

Arrange 5 asparagus spears on each of the six plates, spoon the yellow risotto in an attractive shape next to the asparagus and cover with a fried egg. Serve at once.

FIORI DI ZUCCHINE

Deep-Fried Courgettes and their Flowers

SERVES 6

2 eggs, beaten
100 g (3½ oz) plain flour
200 ml (7 fl oz) milk
salt
18 courgette flowers with about 5 cm (2 in) of courgette attached, washed and dried carefully
oil for deep frying

Mix the eggs, flour, milk and salt to taste together to make a smooth batter. Dip the flowers into the batter to coat them completely. Heat a large pan of oil until a small piece of bread dropped into it sizzles instantly. Fry the courgette flowers for about 30 seconds until crisp and golden brown. Drain on kitchen paper and sprinkle with salt. Serve hot.

Deep fry the courgette flowers in sizzling hot oil for about 30 seconds (below left).

FIORI DI ZUCCHINE (below), *with cherries as a colourful decorative touch.*

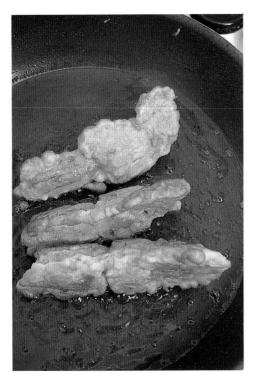

CRESPELLE DI RICOTTA E SPINACI

Ricotta and Spinach Pancakes

SERVES 6

Pancakes (makes 12)
75 g (2½ oz) plain flour
200 ml (7 fl oz) milk
5 eggs
a pinch of salt
75 g (2½ oz) melted butter, cooled
butter or oil for cooking

Filling
250 g (9 oz) ricotta cheese
100 g (3½ oz) cooked spinach, chopped
2 cloves garlic, finely chopped

1 tablespoon fresh parsley, chopped
1 tablespoon fresh basil, chopped
50 g (1¾ oz) Parmesan cheese, freshly grated
1 tablespoon olive oil
salt and freshly milled black pepper

Béchamel Sauce
50 g (1¾ oz) butter
50 g (1¾ oz) plain flour
500 ml (18 fl oz) milk
a pinch of grated nutmeg
a pinch of salt
cheese to taste

First make the pancakes. Beat the flour and milk together until smooth, then beat in the eggs, salt and butter. Stir very thoroughly until the mixture is completely amalgamated and free of lumps. Let it rest for 30 minutes.

In a 17.5 cm (7 in) frying pan, heat about ½ teaspoon of fat, making sure the pan is evenly coated. Stir the batter thoroughly, then pour in just enough to coat the pan evenly. Shake gently and cook for about 1 minute or until the pancake is like paper and just golden on the bottom. Turn over and cook for 1 minute on the other side. Turn out on to a plate. Stack the pancakes interleaved with kitchen paper.

Mix together the filling ingredients and season to taste. Fill the pancakes and fold them into triangles. Arrange them, overlapping slightly, in an ovenproof dish.

To make the béchamel, melt the butter in a heavy-bottomed saucepan until foaming. Add the flour and stir to make a smooth paste which comes away from the sides of the pan.

Meanwhile, heat the milk until just below boiling point. Remove the saucepan with the flour and butter from the heat and gradually stir in the hot milk. Once all the milk has been added, use a whisk to blend the ingredients thoroughly. Return to the heat and continue to cook, stirring constantly with a wooden spoon, until the sauce no longer tastes of flour (about 5 minutes). Stir in the nutmeg and salt and remove from the heat. Add the cheese and return it to the heat for a couple of minutes just to melt the cheese and stir thoroughly.

Pour the sauce over the pancakes. Sprinkle with cheese and breadcrumbs and dot with the butter. Bake in a preheated moderate oven (180°C, 350°F, gas mark 4) for 20–25 minutes, or until golden brown. Serve hot.

CRESPELLE DI RICOTTA E SPINACI (left)

MILANESE STREET (right) *A quiet backwater survives on the edge of the city's bustling centre.*

MOZZARELLA IN CARROZZA

Deep-Fried Mozzarella

SERVES 6

12 slices of white bread, crusts removed
250 ml (9 fl oz) milk (more may be required)
500 g (1 lb 2 oz) mozzarella cheese, sliced
dried oregano
100 g (3½ oz) plain flour
3 eggs, beaten
salt and freshly milled pepper
dried breadcrumbs
oil for deep frying
lettuce, to serve

Dip one side of each slice of bread quickly in the milk, then lay a slice of mozzarella on the dry side of 6 of the slices. Sprinkle the mozzarella with dried oregano and cover with the other 6 slices of bread, dry side inwards, to make sandwiches. Coat the sandwiches in flour, then in the beaten egg which should be seasoned with salt and pepper, and finally in breadcrumbs. Make sure the sides of the 'sandwiches' are well sealed.

Heat a large pan of oil until a small piece of bread dropped into it sizzles instantly. Fry the sandwiches one or two at a time until crisp. Drain on kitchen paper, cut into triangles and serve hot on a bed of lettuce.

STREET MARKET *Because the Milanese expect such high quality in their food and drink, both expensive specialist shops and ordinary markets alike have high standards to meet.*

FICHI VERDI CON ZABAGLIONE DI PROSECCO

Green Figs with Prosecco Zabaglione

SERVES 6

12 ripe green figs
4 egg yolks
4 tablespoons caster sugar
4 tablespoons Prosecco or other sparkling white wine

Slice all the figs in half lengthways. Put the egg yolks, sugar and wine in the top half of a double boiler or in a heatproof bowl placed over a pan of hot water. Whisk over water that is kept just below boiling point until fluffy, light and thickened (about 25 minutes).

Cover 6 large plates with the zabaglione, arrange the cut figs in the middle – 4 half figs on each plate – and chill them until required or serve immediately.

DESIGNER DISHES *Appearances count in Milan – this is after all the home of Italy's best known nouvelle cuisine restaurant – and food is expected to look as good as it tastes.*

MANGIARE IN SPIAGGIA

Eating on the Beach

I am not a great lover of picnic tables and chairs; indeed, they are rarely used for Italian picnics. The exception, however, is for food eaten on the beach. There are few things I find more revolting than grains of sand crunching between one's back teeth – not to mention the amount of work that has gone into preparing food which then becomes inedible. So if we are having lunch on the beach, I always choose a site with tables and chairs, and food that can easily be eaten with the fingers. The only exception in this menu is the *panzanella*, which needs bowls and forks. Everything else can be packed before you set off, then just picked up and eaten.

Most Italian beaches are in fact very well equipped for people wanting to have lunch there. Although many have restaurants of their own, quite often there will be rough wooden tables and chairs set in shady places for those who wish to eat their own food.

You can usually buy drinks from the beach bar, and they will be happy to supply extra forks or plates or whatever you might have forgotten to pack. Many beaches even have a small table next to the brightly coloured beach umbrella and deck chairs which you are able to hire.

When I was younger and more adventurous, we used to have picnics at Cinqueterre. The Cinqueterre is an area near La Spezia in Liguria, made up of five fisher-men's villages which cling precariously to the cliff face and are difficult to get to by land. Here we would picnic not on the usual beaches but in sandy coves that could only be reached by boat. Our boatman was called Guelfo and he would row us out and around the furthermost point in his old wooden boat. When the boat drew level with the appointed spot he would drop anchor and wait while we inflated a small dinghy, into which the picnic and assorted oddments such as suntan oil and footballs would be placed. With flippers on our feet we would then swim in to shore, pushing the dinghy ahead of us with our hands and beaching it on the soft sand. At sunset, after we had enjoyed a wonderfully private day on 'our' beach, we would be collected by Guelfo in the same way. I think I'll have to wait until my children are a little older before I take them on such an adventurous expedition.

Menu

Focaccia con Peperoni

Cotolette di Tacchino

Sedano con il Gorgonzola

Torta Salata

La Panzanella

Albicocche Ripiene di Ricotta e Noci

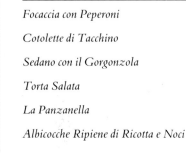

LUNCH BY THE SEA (right) *Shaded tables and chairs are provided on many Italian beaches so you can eat in comfort.*

ALBICOCCHE RIPIENE DI RICOTTA E NOCI (right)

70

FOCACCIA CON PEPERONI

Focaccia with Braised Peppers

SERVES 6

You can buy focaccia ready made in Italy. If you wish, substitute some very crusty bread or pitta for the focaccia.

6 squares or rectangles of focaccia, each about 20 cm (8 in) square
3 large, fleshy peppers, any colour
4 tablespoons olive oil
2 cloves garlic, chopped
salt and freshly milled pepper
butter (optional)

Split each piece of focaccia open to make an envelope. Wash and dry the peppers, cut them in half and remove all seeds and membranes. Slice them into strips. Heat the oil and the garlic together for about 3 minutes, then add the peppers. Stir, then cover and allow to braise gently for about 15 minutes or until soft. Season well. Stir occasionally and add water if necessary.

If the beach is very near, you can put the peppers into the bread envelopes while still warm; otherwise wait until they're completely cold to prevent the bread getting really soggy. If you like, you can spread the bread with butter before filling.

Focaccia is obviously a very convenient picnic bread and can be filled with a huge variety of different fillings. Slices of mozzarella and tomato, prosciutto or cooked mixed vegetables are just a few other suggestions.

COTOLETTE DI TACCHINO

Turkey Escalopes

SERVES 6

12 very thin slices of turkey breast, or 12 small turkey escalopes
2 eggs, beaten
150 g (5 oz) fresh breadcrumbs
oil for frying
salt and freshly milled pepper
lemon wedges

Flatten the turkey slices or escalopes as much as possible with a meat mallet. Put the turkey in the beaten egg, season and leave it to rest for about 1 hour.

Remove the turkey from the egg and let any excess egg drip off, then smother each slice generously in breadcrumbs. Heat 5 cm (2 in) of oil until sizzling and fry all the escalopes until golden brown. They will need about 2 minutes on each side. Drain very thoroughly on kitchen paper.

Serve cold, with lemon wedges to squeeze over them.

FOCACCIA CON PEPERONI

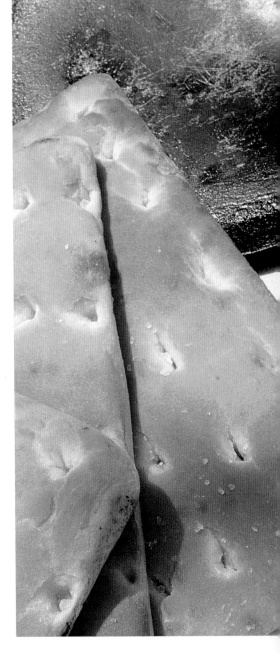

SEDANO CON IL GORGONZOLA

Celery with Gorgonzola

SERVES 6

120 g (4 oz) gorgonzola cheese
250 g (8½ oz) ricotta cheese
2 tablespoons milk (more may be necessary)
1 small onion, finely chopped
a pinch of paprika
salt
2 tablespoons olive oil
2 sprigs celery leaves, finely chopped
12 sticks celery, each cut into 3 sections

Put the gorgonzola into a food processor or blender with the ricotta, milk, chopped onion, paprika and salt to taste. Whizz until blended, then add the oil and the celery leaves.

Wash the celery sticks carefully and make sure they are properly dry. Fill with the cheese mixture and chill until required.

TORTA SALATA

Savoury Pie

SERVES 6

Pastry
300 g (11 oz) plain flour
150 g (5 oz) butter or margarine, softened
1 egg
cold water to mix
salt
Filling
300 g (11 oz) ricotta cheese
200 g (7 oz) fontina or Edam cheese, freshly grated
100 g (3½ oz) butter or margarine, softened
5 eggs, separated

Sift the flour on to the work top in a pile and plunge your fist into the centre to make a hole; put the remaining pastry ingredients into this hole. Blend together quickly with your fingertips to make a soft, elastic ball of dough. Try not to knead the dough as this will make it heavy. Cover with a cloth and put in a cool place to rest for 1 hour.

Meanwhile, sieve the ricotta carefully into a bowl. Add the grated cheese, butter and 5 egg yolks and mix lightly but thoroughly to create an even texture. Whisk the egg whites until stiff and fold into the ricotta mixture.

Butter a 22.5 cm (9 in) flan tin and dust with flour. Roll out three-quarters of the pastry and use to line the tin. Fill it with the ricotta mixture. Roll out the rest of the pastry, cut into strips and use to make a lattice on top.

Bake in a preheated moderately hot oven (190°C, 375°F, gas mark 5) for about 40 minutes or until set and golden brown. Serve cold or just tepid.

LA PANZANELLA

Tomato and Bread Salad

SERVES 6

4 large marmande tomatoes, cut into wedges
2 large onions, finely sliced
1 large cucumber, peeled and cut into cubes
a handful of fresh basil leaves
3 stale white bread rolls, soaked in cold water for about 1 hour
about 6 tablespoons olive oil
3 tablespoons white wine vinegar
salt and freshly milled pepper

Put the tomatoes and onions into a bowl with the cucumber and basil leaves. Mix together with your hands. Take the bread out of the water, squeeze it dry with your hands and mix into the salad. Dress with plenty of olive oil, vinegar and salt and pepper to taste. Toss it all together and leave to stand for at least 2 hours. It is even better if left overnight in the refrigerator.

ALBICOCCHE RIPIENE DI RICOTTA E NOCI

Apricots with Almond and Ricotta Filling

SERVES 6

about 24 almonds
250 g (8½ oz) ricotta cheese
a pinch of ground cinnamon
2 tablespoons caster sugar
12 fresh apricots, carefully stoned but left as intact as possible

Peel and chop finely 12 of the almonds. Mash the ricotta carefully and stir in the cinnamon, chopped almonds and sugar. Fill each apricot carefully with this mixture, then decorate each one with a whole almond on top of the filling and chill until required.

Fresh dates are also very good when stuffed with this filling. A further variation is to substitute walnuts for the almonds.

TORTA SALATA (left)

ALBICOCCHE RIPIENE DI RICOTTA E NOCI (right)

L'ANNIVERSARIO DI NOZZE

Wedding Anniversary Dinner

My brother Howard and his wife Benedetta are the ultimate childhood sweethearts, so their twelfth wedding anniversary was a very special occasion. We decided to hold their anniversary dinner in their favourite restaurant, tucked away in the backstreets of central Milan behind La Scala.

The restaurant looks totally anonymous from the outside and the sign bears no name, just the word Trattoria. Yet once inside you discover the atmosphere of a well-established and serious eating house, the walls decorated with framed napkins upon which the many famous names who have eaten here have either drawn or written a few words.

As the owner is Tuscan, the food has a light and rustic style about it that is light years away from the more heavy-duty Lombard cuisine. Milan, in fact, offers the very best of any regional or international food, if you know where to find it. My brother and his wife are both excellent cooks and fairly passionate gourmets, so one is always guaranteed very good food in their company! This evening turned out to be no

exception – they invited all their closest friends to join them for what proved to be a memorable anniversary banquet.

We began with *capesante gratinate*, a dish of scallops coated with a piquant and delicious grilled topping of anchovies, capers, garlic and breadcrumbs, with the unusual addition of chopped pickled onions for a truly unique flavour. To follow there were *crostini alla Toscana*, toasted Tuscan bread covered with a purée of minced beef and chicken liver. We moved from the antipasti to the first courses – a spectacular seafood spaghetti dish, *spaghetti allo scoglio*, which looked so attractive with many of the shellfish left in their shells, and a light and delicate risotto with courgettes and their flowers.

The next course, *tagliata vegetariana*, looked as good as it tasted. A large platter of paper-thin slices of beef fillet was covered with a selection of vegetables and it was the many different tastes and textures of the dish which made it especially interesting.

The masterpiece of the evening had to be the enormous sea bass,

baked in a covering of rock salt and egg white so that it was as brown on the outside as a loaf of well-baked bread. When the salt crust was split open you could virtually smell the sea as the aroma of the fish, cooked without condiments of any kind, filtered through the cracks. Anyone who had thought they couldn't possibly eat any more needed no further persuasion!

At this point a multi-coloured, multi-flavoured salad with a delicious dressing was served and it was perfect for clearing the way for Franco's dessert speciality: the most wonderfully rich, gooey *tiramisù* I have ever eaten, made with the freshest mascarpone. The lightest possible end to this really superb meal was provided with tiny *fragoline al vino bianco*, wonderful wild strawberries soaked in white wine. Wild strawberries are actually quite common in Italy and they were a delicious finishing touch to linger over before our *espressos*. We all rolled out into the balmy night, feeling replete and knowing we had celebrated the wedding anniversary in the best possible style.

MILAN TRATTORIA *The restaurant where we held Howard and Benedetta's dinner is a real haven, comfortable yet with a serious attitude to the food it serves. We arrived fairly early, as the staff were finishing their own meal.*

Menu

Capesante Gratinate

Crostini alla Toscana

Spaghetti allo Scoglio

Risotto con Zucchine e Fiori

Tagliata Vegetariana

Branzino al Sale

Tiramisù

Fragoline al Vino Bianco

CAPESANTE GRATINATE

Gratin of Scallops

SERVES 6

18 scallops, cleaned and ready to cook
5 tablespoons fresh breadcrumbs
3 tablespoons chopped fresh parsley
2 tablespoons capers, rinsed, dried and chopped
3 canned anchovies, rinsed, dried and chopped
2 cloves garlic, chopped
3 small pickled onions, rinsed, dried and chopped
8 tablespoons olive oil

Lay the scallops, in their half shells, in a flat ovenproof dish. Mix the breadcrumbs with the parsley, capers, anchovies, garlic and pickled onions in a bowl. Add the oil and stir until well mixed. Cover each scallop with a good spoonful of this paste. Place in a preheated moderately hot oven (200°C, 400°F, gas mark 6) and bake for about 15–20 minutes, depending on the size of the scallops, or until crisp on the top. Take care not to overcook them or they will be rubbery. Serve hot.

GARLIC FOR SALE *Straw baskets overflow with freshly picked garlic on this rudimentary market stall in Milan.*

CROSTINI ALLA TOSCANA

Tuscan Toast

SERVES 6

2 cloves garlic, chopped
1 small onion, chopped
3 sprigs of fresh parsley, chopped
4 tablespoons olive oil
100 g (3½ oz) lean beef steak, minced
100 g (3½ oz) chicken livers, minced
½ wineglass of dry red wine
½ wineglass of red wine vinegar
1 tablespoon tomato purée
150 ml (¼ pint) stock or broth
salt and freshly milled pepper
2 tablespoons capers, rinsed, drained and chopped
3 canned anchovies, rinsed, drained and chopped, or
1 heaped tablespoon anchovy paste
thin slices of French or Italian bread, toasted, to
serve

Fry the garlic, onion and parsley together gently in the olive oil until the onion is soft. Add the minced beef and chicken livers and cook until well browned and crumbly.

Pour on the wine and boil to evaporate the alcohol fumes for 2 or 3 minutes. Add the vinegar and boil to evaporate the fumes in the same way. Add the tomato purée and stir carefully. Cook for 8–10 minutes stirring the mixture occasionally.

Stir in the stock and seasoning. Cover and simmer for 1 hour. Ten minutes before serving, stir in the capers and anchovies or anchovy paste.

To serve, spread the mixture on toasted slices of French or Italian bread.

FRESHLY CAUGHT CLAMS *When serving clams in their shells, make sure you scrub the outside and rinse them thoroughly before using.*

SPAGHETTI ALLO SCOGLIO

SPAGHETTI ALLO SCOGLIO

Reef Spaghetti

Ready cooked, fresh shellfish may be used in this dish, but they will need less time to cook.

SERVES 6

5 tablespoons olive oil
3 cloves garlic, finely chopped
1 kg (2¼ lb) mixed shellfish such as clams,
mussels, razorshells, scallops, whelks, cockles, etc.,
including shells, washed and cleaned
salt and freshly milled pepper
1 large wineglass of white wine
2 tablespoons tomato purée
500 g (1 lb 2 oz) spaghetti
3 tablespoons chopped fresh parsley

Heat the oil in a large pan with the garlic until the garlic is golden brown. Season with salt and pepper, then pour in the wine and stir again. Allow the alcohol from the wine to evaporate for 2 or 3 minutes, then add the tomato purée and stir again. Remove the whelks and scallops from their shells, then toss in all the shellfish (which must be scrupulously clean and sand- or grit-free) and mix together thoroughly. Remove from the heat as soon as all the shells have opened up.

Bring a large pot of salted water to the boil, toss in the spaghetti and stir. Cook until the spaghetti is *al dente*, then drain immediately and transfer the spaghetti to the pan with the shellfish. Return to the heat and toss to mix everything together for 2–3 minutes. Sprinkle with parsley and serve at once.

RISOTTO CON ZUCCHINE E FIORI

Risotto with Courgettes and their Flowers

SERVES 6

1.5 litres (2½ pints) vegetable or chicken stock
7 young, tender courgettes, with their flowers if possible
4 tablespoons olive oil
salt and freshly milled pepper
500 g (1 lb 2 oz) risotto rice
15 g (½ oz) unsalted butter
5 tablespoons freshly grated Parmesan cheese

Heat the stock to just below boiling point. Meanwhile, slice the courgettes and their flowers very finely. In a large deep frying pan or wide saucepan, fry the sliced courgettes and flowers until tender in the olive oil. Add the rice and stir it to coat with the oil. Season, then begin to add the hot stock, stirring constantly to prevent sticking. Never add more than one ladleful of liquid at a time and wait for the rice to absorb it before adding any more. (You may not need all the liquid, depending on the quality of the rice.) The rice will take 20 minutes to cook from the time you begin adding the liquid.

Remove from the heat. Adjust the seasoning, stir in the butter and cheese and transfer to a platter to serve.

COURGETTE FLOWERS (left) *The vibrant orange of courgette flowers makes them as attractive to look at as to eat.*

SAUTÉED ARTICHOKES *Artichokes, either on their own or mixed with other vegetables, taste particularly good in* tagliata vegetariana.

TAGLIATA VEGETARIANA

Thinly Sliced Beef Fillet with Mixed Vegetables

SERVES 6

1 whole beef fillet, weighing about 750 g (1¾ lb)
3–4 tablespoons olive oil
salt
freshly milled pepper
500 g (1 lb 2 oz) mixed vegetables cooked separately, such as sautéed artichokes, grilled radicchio, steamed asparagus, sautéed mushrooms, etc., kept warm
(you can have a mixture of vegetables or only one type if you prefer)

Slice the beef fillet as thinly as possible using a very sharp knife (or you could ask your butcher to do this for you). Grease a flat ovenproof dish lightly with a little of the oil, then arrange the meat slices on top in rows, slightly overlapping. Sprinkle the meat with the remaining oil and with salt and freshly milled pepper to taste.

Place in a preheated moderately hot oven (200°C, 400°F, gas mark 6) and roast for about 3 minutes just to seal the meat. This will leave the meat very pink. If you like it medium rare, roast it for 4–5 minutes.

Remove from the oven, cover with all the vegetables to hide the meat completely and serve at once.

An alternative is to serve the cooked mixed vegetables cold with the warm meat. The different textures make an interesting contrast.

Clean the fish carefully and dry both inside and out with kitchen paper.
To cook the fish you will need a large baking dish lined with foil.

BRANZINO AL SALE

Sea Bass Baked in Salt

Grey mullet makes a good alternative to sea bass.

SERVES 6

1 fresh sea bass, weighing about 1.5 kg
(3¼ lb), gutted
1.5 kg (3¼ lb) fine sea salt
5 egg whites
For serving
olive oil
lemon wedges

Wash the fish carefully. Dry it all over, inside and out, with kitchen paper, then lay it in a baking dish lined with foil (cut off the head if it does not fit in the dish).

Mix the salt with the egg whites until you have a smooth, even texture. Cover the fish completely and thickly with the salt mixture. Bake in a preheated moderately hot oven (190°C, 375°F, gas mark 5) for about 40 minutes. When it is ready, it should look like a well-baked loaf of bread.

To serve, break the crust of salt along both sides with a very sharp knife and lift off the top. Lift the fish on to a serving platter and divide into portions. Serve with a little jug of olive oil and some lemon wedges.

Other fish can be cooked in this way, too, as long as they have a thick scaly skin. Mullet and dorade are suitable alternatives.

THE PIÈCE DE RÉSISTANCE *The real high point of the meal was the spectacular* branzino al sale, *or sea bass in its crusty coating of sea salt.*

TIRAMISÙ

Pick Me Up

SERVES 8–10

500 g (1lb 2 oz) mascarpone or rich cream cheese
8 eggs, separated
8 tablespoons caster sugar
1 small cup (100 ml/3½ fl oz) of very strong
espresso coffee
300 ml (½ pint) weak coffee
5 tablespoons brandy
about 30 boudoir biscuits
ground coffee or chocolate powder for dusting

Whisk the mascarpone or cream cheese with a wooden spoon to make it soft and creamy. Beat the egg yolks in a separate bowl until fluffy and pale yellow. Add the sugar to the egg yolks a little at a time until you have a smooth texture, then add this to the cream cheese mixture. Stir in the strong coffee. Whisk the egg whites separately until stiff, then fold them into the cheese, egg and coffee mixture. Set this mixture aside.

Pour the weak coffee and brandy into a bowl. Dip the boudoir biscuits into it one at a time, to moisten them, and arrange the biscuits in a layer in the bottom of a shallow bowl. Cover with some of the cheese mixture, then cover with more moistened biscuits. Continue to make layers in this way until you have used up all the ingredients, ending with a layer of cheese mixture. Sprinkle with the ground coffee or chocolate powder and chill for at least 1 hour or until required.

After whisking the mascarpone to a soft, creamy texture, beat the eggs in a separate bowl. Once they are fluffy and pale yellow, add the sugar to them.

In a shallow dish, make alternate layers of moistened boudoir biscuits and cheese mixture.

FRAGOLINE AL VINO BIANCO

Wild Strawberries with White Wine

SERVES 6

500 g (1 lb 2 oz) wild or alpine strawberries (or
ordinary strawberries cut into small pieces)
3 tablespoons caster sugar
1 wineglass of dry white wine (even better if it's
champagne!)

Hull and wash the strawberries carefully. Dry them and arrange them in a bowl. Sprinkle over the sugar and pour the wine over them. Leave to macerate in the refrigerator for about 2 hours before serving.

Raspberries are also delicious when soaked in wine, particularly a sparkling dry white wine like Italian Prosecco. Prepare them in the same way as strawberries.

Another alternative is the interesting contrast of a sour fruit, such as medlar or citrus fruit, soaked in a sweet white wine such as Asti Spumante.

LA FESTA DELLA RICOTTA

A Feast of Ricotta

I can remember how fascinated I was when I was first taken up into the mountains to watch the shepherds making ricotta. Nowadays most ricotta is made from cow's milk as opposed to the original version which was made exclusively from ewe's milk. It is a very soft, fresh cheese which is used a great deal in Italian cooking both in sweet and savoury dishes, as well as being eaten on its own sprinkled with sugar or cinnamon. As a little girl, my typical *merenda*, tea-time snack, would be a huge slab of bread covered with ricotta and then coated with granulated sugar.

Ricotta is a particularly good partner for fresh spinach and mashed together in *gnocchi* these two ingredients make a wonderful combination. It also crops up in pies, pasta, on pizzas and in pasties. If Parmesan cheese is the king of Italian cheeses then ricotta has to be the queen.

Ricotta forms the basis of the most famous of all Sicilian desserts: *la cassata*. Although this has now become the name for an international ice cream, the original dish is a cake so rich and overpoweringly filling that it could not be from anywhere but Sicily. It is actually fairly simple to make – a casing of sponge cake is filled with a creamy ricotta filling, then decorated with a sumptuously thick icing and candied fruits. Historically, cassata was made by nuns in celebration of Easter, but in time they had to be forbidden from making it because they were neglecting their holy duties for cake making.

Nowadays there seems to be no particular time of year to eat cassata and in Sicily you will be offered it constantly.

The other superb cakes made with ricotta in Sicily are the lovely *cannoli alla Siciliana*. To make these pastries you need a special Sicilian kit of metal or bamboo tubes to keep them perfectly hollow and in shape. The filling – ricotta with icing sugar and candied peel – is incredibly sweet.

If you ever get a chance to taste ricotta that has only just been made and is therefore still warm, you will discover a cheese that is very different indeed from the plastic-wrapped supermarket variety – and you'll be hooked!

Menu

Cannelloni Ripieni di Ricotta e Salsicce

Culigiones

Calzone

Ricotta in Canape

Budino di Ricotta

Crostata di Ricotta

Cassata alla Siciliana

FLOCK OF SHEEP (left)
Traditionally, ricotta is made from ewe's milk, although nowadays most of the ricotta on sale is made with milk from cows.

MAKING RICOTTA (left) *The ricotta-making process varies slightly from region to region, and one can also find salted and smoked versions of the cheese.*

TRADITIONAL RICOTTA PRODUCTION *The word 'ricotta', which literally means 're-cooked', derives from the process by which the cheese is made. First of all, the milk is heated (above and above right) until the whey separates. (Often the curd is used to produce other cheeses.) The whey is then skimmed off and reheated to a high temperature, at which point thicker lumps of whey begin to form on the surface. It is this thickened whey which is in turn skimmed off and put in the traditional wicker baskets which allow it to drain (right). The finished cheese is never aged but is eaten or used fresh. Molise is famous for its top quality cheese, but there are also many other areas in the country producing excellent ricotta.*

CANNELLONI RIPIENI DI RICOTTA E SALSICCE

Cannelloni with a Ricotta and Sausage Filling

SERVES 6

Pasta
250 g (9 oz) plain flour
a pinch of salt
3 eggs
2–3 tablespoons water
Tomato Sauce
45 g (1½ oz) butter or 3 tablespoons olive oil
1 clove garlic, finely chopped
1 small onion, finely chopped
1 small carrot, finely chopped
1 small stick celery, finely chopped
3 tablespoons tomato purée
250 ml (8 fl oz) water
salt and freshly milled pepper
Filling
3 large Italian sausages
500 g (1 lb 2 oz) ricotta cheese
a pinch of salt
1 egg, beaten
5 tablespoons freshly grated Parmesan cheese
To Finish
butter for greasing
5 tablespoons freshly grated Parmesan cheese
45 g (1½ oz) butter, cubed

Make the pasta first. Sift the flour and salt on to the work top in a pile and plunge your fist into the centre to make a hole. Put the eggs and water into the hole. Knead all these together very thoroughly. You can also do this in the food processor. Begin to roll out the dough, then fold it in half and roll out again. Continue to do this until it is smooth and elastic and you hear the air pop out from under the fold as you press down with the rolling pin. Cover the dough with a cloth and put it to one side.

To make the sauce, heat the butter or oil in a saucepan and fry the garlic, onion, carrot and celery until the vegetables are completely soft. Add the tomato purée and water, stir and season to taste. Simmer the tomato sauce gently for about 20–30 minutes.

Put the sausages in a frying pan, prick them all over and cover with cold water. Cook over a low heat until the water has evaporated, then sizzle the sausages in their own fat for 5–6 minutes. Remove from the pan and allow them to cool.

Meanwhile, make the filling. Sieve the ricotta into a bowl and add the salt, egg and grated Parmesan. Stir thoroughly. Skin the sausages and crumble the meat into the ricotta mixture. Stir it all together.

Meanwhile, roll out the pasta dough to a thickness of about 3 mm (1/10 in) and cut into 7 cm (3 in) squares. Bring a very large pot of salted water to the boil and cook the squares 4 at a time for about 1 minute or until they rise to the surface. Scoop them out as soon as they are ready and lay them on the work top or on wet tea towels.

Butter an ovenproof dish carefully. Fill each pasta square with ricotta filling, roll closed and lay them in rows in the ovenproof dish. Sprinkle over the grated Parmesan, scatter the cubes of butter and pour the tomato sauce all over to cover. Bake in a preheated moderately hot oven (190°C, 375°F, gas mark 5) for about 30 minutes. Serve hot.

CULIGIONES

Sardinian Ravioli

SERVES 6

Pasta
500 g (1 lb 2 oz) plain flour
5 eggs
½ teaspoon oil, for oiling rolling pin
Filling
6 heaped tablespoons fresh ricotta cheese
2 large potatoes, peeled, boiled and mashed
5 tablespoons freshly grated Parmesan cheese
3 tablespoons freshly grated pecorino cheese or hard goat's cheese
2 tablespoons chopped fresh mixed herbs
salt and freshly milled pepper
75 g (2½ oz) unsalted butter, melted, to serve

Make the pasta first as on page 87, but without adding any salt or water. Roll out the dough until it is elastic and as thin as possible. (Rub the oil on the rolling pin to help you roll.)

Cut the pasta into 24 squares, each about 10 cm (4 in) per side. Cover with a cloth while you quickly prepare the filling.

Sieve the ricotta into a bowl and mix it with the potatoes, cheeses and herbs. Season with salt and pepper.

Place about 1 tablespoon filling on 12 of the pasta squares and cover with the other 12 squares. Press the edges closed securely to seal the filling inside.

Bring a large pot of salted water to a rolling boil and slip the squares into the water. Cook for 4–5 minutes, then remove with a fish slice. Arrange 2 ravioli on each of 6 warm plates. Cover each portion with melted butter and serve at once.

CALZONE

Stuffed pizza

SERVES 6

Dough

350 g (13 oz) plain flour
15 g (½ oz) fresh yeast
300 ml (½ pint) warm water
a pinch of sugar
2 tablespoons olive oil
a pinch of salt
oil for greasing

Filling

10 canned anchovy fillets, drained
6 sun-dried tomatoes
225 g (8 oz) ricotta cheese

Pile the flour on the work top and plunge your fist into the centre to make a hole. Crumble the yeast into the centre and add the sugar. Using a fork, blend enough water into the yeast to make a smooth paste. Then gradually add more water as necessary and knead the flour, yeast and sugar mixture together very thoroughly with your hands. About halfway through the kneading add the salt and oil.

Continue to knead the dough until it is smooth and elastic. Then place the ball of dough in a lightly floured bowl and cover it with a lightly floured cloth. Place in a warm spot for about 2½ hours, when it should have doubled in volume.

CALZONE (left)

Meanwhile, make the filling. Rinse the anchovy fillets then chop the anchovies and the tomatoes into small pieces and mix with the ricotta. Set aside until required.

When the dough has doubled in volume, remove it from the bowl and divide it into 6 pieces. Flatten each piece into a disc shape about 0.5 cm (¼ in) thick. Place filling in the middle of the dough then fold the dough in half and seal the edges carefully with your fingers. Place the *calzone* on an oiled baking sheet and bake in a preheated hot oven (200°C, 400°F, gas mark 6) for 20 minutes or until golden brown. Brush the surface with olive oil and serve hot.

RICOTTA IN CANAPE

Ricotta with Eggs

SERVES 6

500 g (1 lb 2 oz) ricotta cheese, cut into 6 slices
55 g (2 oz) butter
6 eggs
6 tablespoons passata (sieved tomatoes)
a large pinch of dried mixed herbs
salt and freshly milled pepper
6 tablespoons freshly grated Parmesan
or other cheese

Fry the slices of ricotta in the butter until just browned on both sides. Lay them in an ovenproof dish. Break the eggs on top and cover with the *passata*. Sprinkle with the herbs, salt and pepper to taste and grated Parmesan. Bake in a preheated moderately hot oven (200°C, 400°F, gas mark 6) for 15 minutes or until the eggs have set. Serve hot.

BUDINO DI RICOTTA

Ricotta Pudding

SERVES 6

300 ml (½ pint) cold water
50 g (2 oz) semolina
400 g (14 oz) fresh ricotta cheese
4 tablespoons caster or icing sugar
1 egg
1 egg yolk
1 heaped tablespoon chopped mixed candied peel
1 heaped tablespoon sultanas
1–2 tablespoons dark rum
1 egg white
butter for greasing
a handful of dried breadcrumbs or semolina
4 tablespoons icing or vanilla sugar, to finish

Bring the water to the boil, then sprinkle in the semolina very slowly, stirring constantly to prevent lumps. It will thicken very quickly. When it is thick and smooth, remove from the heat and tip into a bowl. Leave to cool.

Mash the ricotta with the sugar, egg, egg yolk, candied peel, sultanas and rum. Blend in the semolina. Whisk the egg white until stiff and fold it into the mixture.

Butter a 1.5 litre (2½ pint) soufflé dish thoroughly and coat it carefully with breadcrumbs or semolina. Tip it upside down to remove the loose crumbs. Pour the pudding mixture into the dish, making sure it comes no more than two-thirds of the way up the sides.

Bake in a preheated oven (180°C, 350°F, gas mark 4) for 45 minutes–1 hour or until golden brown. Turn the pudding out on to a platter. Cover with sifted icing or vanilla sugar and serve warm or cold.

CROSTATA DI RICOTTA

Ricotta Flan

SERVES 6

Pastry
200 g (7 oz) plain flour
4 tablespoons cornflour
2½ tablespoons sifted icing sugar
150 g (5 oz) unsalted butter
grated rind of 1 lemon
Custard
2 tablespoons caster sugar
2 egg yolks
1 tablespoon plain flour
300 ml (½ pint) milk
Filling
300 g (11 oz) ricotta cheese
3 eggs, separated
3 tablespoons caster sugar
a large pinch of ground cinnamon
3 tablespoons chopped mixed candied peel
To Finish
butter for greasing
1 egg, beaten
4 tablespoons vanilla sugar

Make the pastry. Sift the flour, cornflour and icing sugar into a bowl and add the butter and lemon rind. Blend everything together quickly with your fingertips or 2 knives to make a smooth, light dough. Don't knead it or it will be heavy. Add a little water if necessary. Rest under a cloth for about 30 minutes.

Next make the custard. Mix the caster sugar, egg yolks and flour together in a heavy-bottomed saucepan until completely smooth. Add the milk and place over the heat. Cook, stirring constantly, until the custard thickens and coats the back of the spoon. Cool.

For the filling, mix the ricotta in a bowl with the egg yolks, sugar, cinnamon and peel. Stir in the cooled custard. Whisk the egg whites until stiff and fold into the mixture.

Roll out about two-thirds of the pastry and use to line a buttered flan tin with a removable base (or a flan ring placed on a baking sheet). Pour the ricotta filling into the pastry case. Roll out the remaining pastry, cut it into strips and lay over the filling to make a lattice. Brush the pastry with beaten egg.

Bake in a preheated moderate oven (180–190°C, 350–375°C, gas mark 4–5) for about 35 minutes or until golden brown. When the flan is baked, remove it from the tin and let it cool. Dust the top of the flan with vanilla sugar just before serving.

CASSATA ALLA SICILIANA (opposite, left) *and* CANNOLI ALLA SICILIANA (opposite, right) *The latter are delicious little pastries with a rich filling of ricotta and candied orange peel.*

CASSATA ALLA SICILIANA

Sicilian Cassata Cake

SERVES 6

550 g (20 oz) fresh ricotta cheese
200 g (7 oz) icing sugar, sifted
1 teaspoon vanilla essence
4 tablespoons maraschino liqueur
4 tablespoons chocolat pâtissier, finely chopped
4 tablespoons chopped mixed candied or glacé fruit
300g (10 oz) sponge cake, thinly sliced
To decorate
assorted glacé fruits
Icing
100 g (3½ oz) icing sugar, sifted
1 tablespoon cold water
2 tablespoons maraschino liqueur

Sieve the ricotta into a bowl and beat in the icing sugar and vanilla essence to make a smooth, light and fluffy texture. Stir in the liqueur, chocolate and candied fruit.

Use the cake slices to line the sides and bottom of a 15 cm (6 in) cake tin, using some of the ricotta mixture to help stick the cake to the tin if it slips. Put the ricotta cream into the lined cake tin, smooth the surface and cover the top with more cake. Chill for about 1 hour or until set slightly.

Turn out the cake on to a platter. To make the icing, mix the icing sugar with the water and liqueur until silky smooth, then spread all over the cake. Chill again to set the icing. Decorate with lots of glacé fruit to serve. Keep chilled until required.

NOZZE SICILIANE

A Wedding in Sicily

Give any Italian an excuse for celebrating and it's guaranteed that they will push the boat out. If they are Sicilian, you can bet whatever you like that they will do it more extravagantly and with more pomp and circumstance than any other Italian. A wedding has to be the very best reason for a celebration and the Sicilians certainly lived up to their reputation on the day Luisa and Marco were married in Palermo.

The wedding reception was held on the wide, Baroque terraces of Palermo's sumptuous Palazzo Butera. It was such an amazing setting for a wedding, with views over the roof tops of the city and the atmosphere of grandeur and elegance which the old *palazzi* always seem to impose. I was amazed at the smooth running of the operation – there were so many staff to organize, before one even thought about the guests or the bride and groom. Yet everything was elegantly colour coordinated, from the yellow and white tablecloths through to the parcels of sugared almonds wrapped in white tulle and decorated with tiny sprigs of yellow mimosa.

There were actually about fifty different things to eat and I have selected ten of my favourites for the menu here to give you a taste of the day. As well as all the food laid out on the buffet, there were three cooks/craftsmen who were stationed on the terrace to provide additional delicacies. They were the *poliparo* – the 'octopus man' who prepared grilled octopus on a barbecue, as well as fish kebabs and other delicacies on request; the *friggitore*, or frier, presided over a huge cauldron of boiling oil and fried all manner of fish and vegetables; the *focacciere* had the job of preparing pizzas and focaccia.

All Italians take their food very seriously, but at a wedding feast they really do throw all thought of calorie counting and cholesterol levels to the wind. If you are ever invited to an Italian wedding, the only strategy is simply to join in the general feeling of, 'Oh, well, there's always tomorrow to recover,' and just enjoy the day. The first time I attended a wedding was in the Abruzzi, in central Italy, where they really do these things properly. We began to eat at about midday and didn't actually get up from the table until well past seven o'clock in the evening. At this point we followed the happy, if extremely full, couple on foot back to the house where they were to spend their first wedding night, heckling them and throwing sugared almonds at them all the way there!

Luisa and Marco's wedding ended on a rather more sedate note, with an incredible sunset which painted the sky every shade of orange and red over the roofs of Palermo.

WAITING IN THE WINGS (left) An army of waiters took care of the large number of guests.

Menu

Sarde a Beccafico

Peperoni Arrosto

Melanzane Fritte in Insalata

Pesce alla Matalotta

Pollo alla Cacciatora con Melanzane

Cazzilli

Cassata Gelata alla Siciliana

Spuma Gelata di Pesche

Gelatina di Mandorle

Granita di Caffè con Panna

CONFETTI OF SUGARED ALMONDS (left) are given to guests by the bride and groom.

SARDE A BECCAFICO

Sicilian Sardines with Oranges

SERVES 8

1.5 kg (3¼ lb) large fresh sardines
150 ml (¼ pint) olive oil
200 g (7 oz) breadcrumbs
100 g (3½ oz) sultanas, soaked in cold water
for 15 minutes
100 g (3½ oz) pine kernels
4 tablespoons chopped fresh parsley
grated rind of 1 orange
juice of 2 oranges
2 teaspoons anchovy paste
bay leaves
1 orange, thinly sliced
salt and freshly milled pepper

Open up the sardines and gut them, then pull out the spine from the tail end, taking the head of each fish with the spine. Wash the headless, gutted fish carefully and pat dry.

Heat about two-thirds of the oil in a frying pan until very hot and add all but 1 tablespoon of the breadcrumbs. Brown carefully all over, then tip into a bowl. Add the drained sultanas, the pine kernels, parsley, orange rind and juice and anchovy paste. Season to taste. Mix all this together and use it to stuff the fish.

Oil an ovenproof dish and lay the stuffed fish in the dish, inserting a bay leaf between each one. Pour the remaining oil over the top and sprinkle over the reserved breadcrumbs. Bake in a preheated oven (180°C, 350°F, gas mark 4) for 30 minutes. Serve hot or cold, garnished with the orange.

PEPERONI ARROSTO

Grilled Peppers

SERVES 8

6 large, fleshy peppers of assorted colours
150 ml (¼ pint) olive oil
2 cloves garlic, very finely chopped
1 tablespoon chopped fresh parsley
salt
freshly milled pepper

Cut the peppers in half, carefully remove all the seeds and membranes and cut the peppers into wide strips.

Place the strips under a preheated medium grill to soften and brown slightly on both sides (they can go a bit black if you like).

Lay the pepper strips in a wide platter and pour over the oil. Sprinkle with the chopped garlic and parsley and season generously with salt and pepper. Serve warm or cold.

PEPERONI ARROSTO (above), *with a simple dressing of olive oil.*

MELANZANE FRITTE IN INSALATA

Fried Aubergine Salad

SERVES 8

300–450 ml (½–¾ pint) olive oil or vegetable oil
4 large aubergines, cut into finger-thick slices

Dressing
a large pinch of dried oregano
4 tablespoons red wine vinegar
5 tablespoons olive oil
salt and freshly milled pepper

Heat the oil in a large frying pan until sizzling hot, then fry the aubergine slices until well browned and slightly crisp on both sides. Drain carefully on kitchen paper, then arrange on a large platter. Pour over the dressing. Leave for at least 30 minutes before serving to allow the flavours to develop.

SARDE A BECCAFICO (left)

MELANZANE FRITTE IN INSALATA (left)

PESCE ALLA MATALOTTA

Fish Casserole with Olives

SERVES 8

1.5 kg (3¼ lb) any firm-fleshed fish, gutted
1 large onion, thinly sliced
150 ml (5 fl oz) olive oil
3 cloves garlic, finely chopped
500 ml (18 fl oz) passata (sieved tomatoes), or 3
tablespoons tomato purée diluted in 500 ml
(18 fl oz) warm water
2 heaped tablespoons capers, rinsed and dried
200 g (7 oz) green olives, stoned and halved
salt and freshly milled black pepper
a handful of fresh parsley, chopped
8 fresh basil leaves
a small handful of fresh celery leaves

Wash and dry the fish carefully. If they are small, leave them whole; if they are large, cut them into even chunks.

Fry the onion in the olive oil in a large pan until soft, then add the garlic, *passata*, capers and olives. Season to taste. Stir the ingredients together, then add the fish and the herbs. Spoon the sauce all over the fish.

Cover and simmer very gently for about 30 minutes without stirring again. Serve hot.

THE BARBECUE (left) *provided additional, piping-hot delicacies.*

BAROQUE SPLENDOUR (right) *The grandeur of the Palazzo Butera provided a sumptuous backdrop.*

POLLO ALLA CACCIATORA CON MELANZANE

Chicken with Aubergines

SERVES 8

4 large aubergines, cut into finger-thick slices
salt and freshly milled pepper
8 chicken joints
4 tablespoons olive oil
3 cloves garlic, chopped
6 rashers streaky bacon or pancetta
300 ml (10 fl oz) dry white wine
400 g (14 oz) canned tomatoes, chopped
oil for deep frying
3 tablespoons chopped fresh parsley

Put the aubergine slices in a large colander and sprinkle generously with salt. Cover with a plate with a weight on top and leave to drain in the sink for 1–2 hours to remove all the bitter juices.

Meanwhile, trim the chicken joints. Heat the olive oil in a large, wide pan and fry the chicken joints quickly with the garlic and bacon or *pancetta*, to brown them all over. Pour the wine over the chicken and allow to evaporate for about 3 minutes, then add the tomatoes. Stir together and season to taste. Cover and simmer for about 35 minutes.

Wipe dry the aubergine slices carefully and deep fry them in hot oil until tender and golden brown. Drain on kitchen paper. Stir them into the chicken dish and cook for a further 5–10 minutes. Transfer to a serving dish, sprinkle with the parsley and serve.

CAZZILLI

Sicilian Potato Fritters

SERVES 8

1 kg (2¼ lb) potatoes suitable for mashing
50 g (1¾ oz) cooked ham
a large handful of fresh parsley
50 g (1¾ oz) butter, softened
4 egg yolks
salt
50 g (1¾ oz) caciocavallo or provolone cheese,
cubed
50 g (1¾ oz) pecorino cheese, freshly grated
3–6 tablespoons plain flour
4 egg whites, beaten until fluffy
125–175 g (4½–6 oz) fresh breadcrumbs
oil for deep frying

Put the unpeeled potatoes in a pan of cold water, bring to the boil and cook for 30 minutes. While the potatoes are cooking, chop the ham and parsley together.

Drain the potatoes and peel them while they are still hot. Push them through a mouli into a clean saucepan to make a smooth purée. While the purée is still warm, stir the butter into the puréed potato. Allow it to cool, then stir in the egg yolks, mixing well. Season to taste with salt and add the chopped ham and parsley and the cubed cheese. Stir in the pecorino, and adjust seasoning as required.

Shape the mixture into 14–16 cylinders with your hands. Coat the cylinders in flour, then in egg white and then in breadcrumbs.

Heat a large pan of oil until a piece of bread dropped into it sizzles instantly. Deep fry the *cazzilli*, a few at a time, until golden and crisp. Drain and serve piping hot.

CASSATA GELATA ALLA SICILIANA

Ice Cream Cassata

SERVES 8

600 g (1¼ lb) best quality vanilla ice cream,
soft enough to spread
300 ml (½ pint) whipping cream
5 tablespoons caster sugar
75 g (2½ oz) chopped mixed glacé fruit
75 g (2½ oz) toasted almonds, chopped
50 g (1¾ oz) good quality plain chocolate, chopped

Line the sides and the bottom of a 1.1 litre (2 pint) bombe mould or pudding basin (preferably metal) with the ice cream. Make sure the centre remains empty so you can fill it with the other ingredients. Place the mould in the freezer to harden the ice cream.

Whip the cream with the caster sugar, then fold in the glacé fruit, almonds and chocolate. Spoon this mixture into the hollow in the ice cream mould. Cover with greaseproof paper and place the lid tightly on top of the mould, sealing the cracks with softened butter. If you don't have a mould with a lid, use foil or clingfilm but do remember to seal it very carefully. Bang the mould firmly on the work top to make everything settle evenly. Freeze for about 2 hours. To serve, dip the mould in hot water for a few seconds and turn out the cassata on to a platter.

ON THE TERRACE *More than fifty dishes were served – truly characteristic of this extravagant island with its colourful, complex, exuberant cuisine.*

SPUMA GELATA DI PESCHE

Frozen Peach Dessert

SERVES *8*

15 g (½ oz) sheet or powdered gelatine
1.5 kg (3¼ lb) yellow peaches, peeled and stoned
juice of 1 large lemon
180 g (6 oz) caster sugar
3 tablespoons maraschino liqueur
150 ml (¼ pint) whipping cream, whipped
until stiff
sliced peaches, to decorate

Cover the gelatine sheets with cold water and allow to soak for about 10–15 minutes or until soft, then drain and squeeze them dry in your hands. Put them in a small saucepan with 3 tablespoons fresh cold water and heat, stirring, until completely dissolved. (If using powdered gelatine, follow the packet instructions.)

Push the peaches through a mouli to make a smooth purée. Stir in the lemon juice, sugar and maraschino liqueur. Add the gelatine to the peach mixture and stir well. Fold in the whipped cream carefully.

Pour the mixture into a freezerproof bowl and place in the freezer. Freeze for at least 2 hours, removing the dessert every 15 or 20 minutes and stirring it thoroughly.

Transfer into individual ice cream bowls and decorate with sliced peaches to serve.

AFTER THE CEREMONY (above) *Sicilians have a huge capacity for celebrating – and what better occasion could there be than a wedding.*

OUTSIDE THE CHURCH *As the couple leave the church, the guests throw rice at them.*

GELATINA DI MANDORLE

Almond Jelly

SERVES *8*

350 g (12 oz) blanched almonds
750 ml (1¼ pints) milk
350 g (12 oz) caster sugar
25 g (1 oz) sheet or powdered gelatine
3 tablespoons dark rum
250 ml (8 fl oz) whipping cream,
whipped until stiff
almond oil for greasing
toasted almonds, to decorate

Pound the almonds in a mortar until finely crushed, gradually adding a little cold water to prevent the almonds exuding any oil. (If you do this in a food processor be very careful not to allow them to get oily.) Put the almonds in a bowl with the milk and stir together carefully. As soon as the almonds are virtually dissolved into the milk, strain the milk into a bowl through muslin, squeezing the muslin very tightly. (You may need to get somebody to help you do this.)

Add the caster sugar to the almond milk and stir until it is completely dissolved. Cover the sheet gelatine with cold water and leave to soak for about 10–15 minutes or until soft, then drain and squeeze the sheets dry with your hands. Put in a little saucepan and stir over a low heat until melted. (If using powdered gelatine, follow the instructions on the packet.) Whisk the gelatine into the almond mixture and stir well. Stir in the rum, and fold in the whipped cream.

Oil a 1.5 litre (2½ pint) mould with almond oil, tipping it upside down to remove any excess. Pour the mixture into the mould and chill for 2–3 hours or until set.

Dip the mould into boiling water for a few seconds and turn out on to a platter. (If you don't want to turn it out of the mould, chill it in an unoiled glass bowl.) Decorate with toasted almonds to serve.

GRANITA DI CAFFÈ CON PANNA

Coffee Sorbet with Whipped Cream

SERVES *8*

200 g (7 oz) caster sugar
500 ml (18 fl oz) cold water
600 ml (1 pint/6 small espresso cups) of very
strong espresso coffee
300 ml (½ pint) whipping cream
4 tablespoons icing sugar, sifted
sugar coffee beans, to decorate

Dissolve the sugar in the water over a low heat. Transfer to a bowl and stir in the coffee. Leave to cool.

Pour into a shallow metal tray and freeze for 2–3 hours. Stir occasionally during this time to prevent the granita becoming too icy. Whip the cream and fold in the icing sugar. Remove the granita from the freezer and spoon into individual dishes. Top with the whipped cream and decorate with sugar coffee beans just before serving.

UN PRANZO A BASE DE PESCE

Seafood Lunch

The southern Italian diet is one of the healthiest in the world. If you set aside for a moment the dreadfully rich desserts, and look at the standard everyday fare, what you come up with is very little meat, lots of vegetables and salads, olive oil instead of butter and plenty of pasta and fruit. When visiting friends in Palermo recently, I expressed a craving for the incredibly fresh, perfumed fish which seemed to be on offer everywhere. Before I knew it, a wonderful roof-top lunch, with lovely views down to the beach, had been arranged for me. I still can't quite get over how willing Italians are to demonstrate at a moment's notice just how wonderful their food is.

Basking in the warm spring sunshine, we enjoyed the very best that the incredibly blue sea down below had to offer. We began with langoustines, then moved on to the ubiquitous *pasta con le sarde*. This is the most typical of all Sicilian pasta dishes

UP ON THE ROOF (right) *From our table on the roof terrace we could see over to the harbour of Palermo.*

and is made to different recipes on the east and west coasts. As an alternative, there was *vermicelli alla Siracusana*, dressed with all the typical flavours of the south. A selection of imaginative flavour combinations followed: octopus stewed with mushrooms, a delicately flavoured prawn stew, and fresh baked whiting.

After this wonderful meal, there was only one thing left to do, and that was to wander slowly down to the beach to see how cold the water was, and maybe have an ice cream on the way. . . .

Menu

Scampi Arrosto

Pasta con le Sarde

Vermicelli alla Siracusana

Polpetti in Umido con Funghi

Gamberi in Intingolo

Nasello alla Palermitana

Gelato all'Amarena con il Mango

FISHING BOATS (right) *The seas around Sicily yield many succulent fish, from tiny anchovies to swordfish.*

SCAMPI ARROSTO

Roasted Langoustines

SERVES 6

2 kg (4½ lb) langoustines or lobster
200 g (7 oz) fresh breadcrumbs (white part of the bread only)

salt and freshly milled pepper
3 tablespoons chopped fresh parsley
4 tablespoons olive oil
grated rind of 1 lemon
lemon wedges, to serve

Ask your fishmonger to prepare the langoustines for you. Wash them thoroughly, then using a very sharp pair of scissors make an incision down the belly from head to tail.

Mix the breadcrumbs with salt, pepper, the parsley, about two-thirds of the oil and the lemon rind. Fill the incision in each langoustine with this mixture.

Arrange the stuffed langoustines carefully on a wire rack over a roasting tin. Brush them with the rest of the oil and bake in a preheated moderately hot oven (180°C, 350°F, gas mark 4) for about 20 minutes.

Serve hot, with wedges of lemon.

PASTA CON LE SARDE

Pasta with Sardines

SERVES 6

400 g (14 oz) fresh sardines
6–7 large sprigs of fennel
salt
freshly milled pepper
1 large onion, finely chopped
100 ml (3½ fl oz) olive oil
1 sachet of saffron powder, diluted in a little hot
water
40 g (1½ oz) pine kernels
40 g (1½ oz) seedless raisins, soaked in cold water
for 15 minutes
1 tablespoon anchovy paste
500 g (1 lb 2 oz) bucatini or similar pasta, such as
uncut macaroni

Open up and gut the sardines carefully, draw-ing out the spine and thus removing the head, but keeping them otherwise intact. (Or ask your fishmonger to do this for you.) Rinse and dry them and set to one side.

Put the fennel in a saucepan with about 2 litres (3½ pints) of water and some salt, bring to the boil and boil until soft. Remove the fennel from the water, drain and chop it finely. Keep the water because you will need it to cook the pasta in.

Put the onion into a wide saucepan, cover with cold water and cook until soft. Add about two-thirds of the olive oil, the saffron, pine kernels and drained and dried raisins. Stir and cook together for about 10 minutes, then add the sardines. Cook for about 10 more minutes, turning the sardines over about halfway through, then add the chopped fennel.

Meanwhile, put the anchovy paste and the remaining oil in a separate pan and simmer over a low heat for about 5 minutes or until reduced to a runny paste.

Return the pot of fennel-flavoured water to the heat and bring to the boil. Toss in the pasta and cook until *al dente* (check packet for cooking time as brands vary).

Drain the pasta, put it into a bowl with the sardine sauce and anchovy paste and toss everything together. Add salt and/or freshly milled pepper to taste. Leave to rest for about 3 minutes before serving.

MENDING NETS *The fishing industry is important to Sicily's economy.*

SCAMPI ARROSTO (far left)

VERMICELLI ALLA SIRACUSANA

Vermicelli with the Sauce of Syracuse

SERVES 6

1 very large yellow pepper or 2 smaller ones
75 ml (3 fl oz) olive oil
2 cloves garlic, chopped
1 tablespoon anchovy paste
400 g (14 oz) canned tomatoes, drained and cut
into small cubes
1 very large aubergine, cut into small cubes
75 g (2½ oz) green olives, coarsely chopped
8 large black olives, coarsely chopped
8 leaves fresh basil, torn to shreds
1 heaped tablespoon capers, rinsed and chopped
salt
500 g (1 lb 2 oz) vermicelli or spaghetti
freshly grated pecorino cheese to taste

Hold the pepper on a long-handled fork over a flame, turning it to blister the skin all over. (Alternatively, grill it.) Rub the skin off, then cut the pepper in half and discard seeds and membranes. Cut into thin strips.

Heat the oil in a saucepan over a medium heat and add the garlic, anchovy paste and the cubed tomatoes and aubergine. Stir and cook for 5 or 6 minutes, then add the green and black olives, basil, pepper strips and capers, and season with salt. Stir and cover. Leave to simmer for 20–25 minutes.

Bring a large pot of salted water to the boil, toss in the pasta and cook until just *al dente*. Drain. Mix the sauce with the pasta, sprinkle with the pecorino and serve at once.

POLPETTI IN UMIDO CON FUNGHI

Stewed Octopus with Mushrooms

SERVES 6

1.5 kg (3 ¼ lb) octopus (young and small if possible)
2 salted anchovies, or 4 canned anchovy fillets, cleaned and rinsed thoroughly
1 clove garlic
a small handful of fresh parsley
4 tablespoons red wine
100 ml (3½ fl oz) olive oil
1 tablespoon tomato purée
salt and freshly milled pepper
50 g (2 oz) dried funghi porcini, soaked in warm water for 15–20 minutes

Clean the octopus, removing the skin, beak, eyes and sacs. (Or ask your fishmonger to do this for you.) Cut it into even, small sections and rinse it until it becomes completely white. Chop together the anchovies, garlic and parsley. Mix with the red wine.

Heat the oil in a heavy-bottomed pan and add the anchovy and garlic mixture. Stir and cook together for about 3 minutes, then stir in the tomato purée. Add the octopus sections and season with plenty of salt and pepper. Cover and simmer for about 45 minutes. Check occasionally and add more water if the stew appears to be drying out.

Drain the *funghi porcini* and rinse them thoroughly. Add them to the stew, cover the pan again and cook for a further 20 minutes. Serve hot.

GAMBERI IN INTINGOLO

Stewed Prawns

SERVES 4–6

30 g (1 oz) butter
1 tablespoon olive oil
1 onion, chopped
1 carrot, chopped
4 sprigs of fresh parsley, chopped
1 kg (2¼ lb) raw prawns, shells removed
salt and freshly milled pepper
150 ml (5 fl oz) dry white wine
2 tablespoons tomato purée
1 tablespoon plain flour
4 slices of white bread, crusts removed
vegetable oil for frying

Heat half the butter and all the olive oil in a frying pan and fry the onion, carrot and parsley until soft. Add the prawns and stir together carefully. Season with salt and pepper and add the wine. As soon as the wine has evaporated remove from the heat.

Take the heads off all the prawns and set the prawns aside. Put the heads in a food processor or mortar. Add the tomato purée and a few tablespoons of hot water and press or pound the heads to make a smooth purée. Pour this purée into a saucepan and add the vegetable mixture. Knead the remaining butter to a paste with the flour and add to the pan. Bring to the boil, stirring constantly, until thickened. Add the prawns and stir to heat through.

Cut the bread into small triangles and fry in the hot oil until crisp.

Arrange the prawns in the centre of a dish and garnish with the bread around the edge. Serve at once.

NASELLO ALLA PALERMITANA

Whiting Cooked in the Style of Palermo

This dish can also be prepared with small mackerel.

SERVES 6

1 large whiting or individual whitings, weighing about 1.25 kg (2 ¾ lb) in total, gutted
olive oil
fresh rosemary
salt and freshly milled pepper
5 teaspoons anchovy paste, or 5 salted or canned anchovies, rinsed and cleaned
4 tablespoons dried breadcrumbs

Rub the inside of the fish carefully with oil. Insert a small branch of rosemary inside each fish and sprinkle the inside of the fish with salt and pepper. Oil an ovenproof dish and lay the fish in it.

Put about 4 tablespoons of oil in a small saucepan and add the anchovy paste or cleaned anchovies. Cook and mash this mixture with a fork to reduce to a smooth purée. Pour this over and inside the fish. Sprinkle with the breadcrumbs and a few leaves of rosemary and a little more salt and pepper.

Place the dish in a preheated moderate oven (170°C, 325°F, gas mark 3) and bake for about 30 minutes. Serve hot.

GELATO ALL'AMARENA CON IL MANGO

GELATO ALL'AMARENA CON IL MANGO

Mangoes with Cherry Ice Cream

SERVES 6

Ice Cream
500 g (1lb 2 oz) very ripe fresh cherries
500 ml (18 fl oz) whipping cream
4–5 tablespoons caster sugar
120 g (4 oz) icing sugar

6 small mangoes

To make the ice cream, stone the cherries and reduce them to a purée in a blender or food processor. Whip the cream with the caster sugar until stiff.

Fold the cream into the cherry purée and add the icing sugar very gradually, folding it in carefully. Transfer to a shallow metal tray and freeze for about 2 hours, taking it out and whisking it energetically every 30 minutes.

Next prepare the mangoes. With a very sharp knife, make 8 cuts through the skin and flesh of each mango, working lengthways from top to bottom but not cutting right through at the end with the stalk attached. Then pull back each segment to achieve the effect of an open flower. Cut out the stone, removing with it as little flesh as possible.

Place each mango on a plate. Cut the flesh away from each 'petal', by sliding a knife between the skin and the fruit three-quarters of the way down. Chill until required. To serve, fill the centre of each 'flower' with ice cream.

UNA FESTA TRA AMICI

Just a Party

In a huge, ancient garden in Tuscany, filled with thin, crooked pine trees, stands a blue-shuttered house – La Dogana Estense. This used to be my grandparents' house when my grandfather was in government and during the summer it was always used to entertain their many friends. Sadly, I never knew my grandparents, but my uncle inherited the villa and continued the tradition of using it as a summer house to which all his friends and acquaintances would be invited.

Apart from the delicious food which was always prepared for these occasions, my most lasting impression of those parties was of their relaxed, casual air. I remember such good conversations and guests who were content simply to enjoy the house, the company, the wonderful food and wine. The villa seemed to assume the role of a miniature gastronomic centre with incredible ease and the atmosphere of unruffled elegance and pleasure has seeped into the walls themselves. It is to this day the best place to have a party and I was delighted to be able to borrow it for one of my own gatherings.

I knew I had to devise a menu that was worthy of the loveliness

LA DOGANA ESTENSE (left)
Wonderful food and good conversation are what I have always associated with my grandparents' house.

of the setting, so I decided to recreate some of the dishes I remember enjoying here on other occasions when I was not the hostess. I arranged all the dishes as a buffet and allowed everybody to

help themselves, beginning with the antipasti and first courses. I then served a tender joint of veal threaded through with pistachio nuts and as an alternative for vegetarians, or accompanying

vegetables for meat eaters, there was a layered dish of courgettes with mozzarella, tomato and basil. The huge tomato salad was dressed with pesto sauce and had pine kernels scattered over it for added crunch.

After a pause I served my two desserts: a light and cooling raspberry bavarois and the most authentic *zuppa inglese* I could muster. The conversation flowed all around me, the wine seemed to match the dishes to perfection – I retired, certain that my grandparents would have been proud of me.

Menu

Insalata di Mozzarella, Olive e Rucola

Gamberi con i Fagioli

Penne al Gorgonzola

Corona di Riso con il Granchio

Pomodori in Insalata con il Pesto e i Pinoli

Arrosto di Vitello con Pistacchi

Parmigiana di Zucchine

Bavarese al Lampone

La Zuppa Inglese

BAVARESE AL LAMPONE (left)

INSALATA DI MOZZARELLA, OLIVE E RUCOLA

Mozzarella Salad with Black Olives and Rocket

SERVES 6

500 g (1 lb 2 oz) mozzarella cheese, well drained
100 g (3½ oz) large black olives, stoned
2 large handfuls of rocket, trimmed, washed and
torn into pieces
9 tablespoons olive oil
salt and freshly milled pepper

Cut the mozzarella into cubes about the size of a cherry. Mix with the olives and rocket leaves in a bowl. Pour over the olive oil and season with salt and pepper. Toss everything together carefully, using 2 spoons. Leave to stand for about 1 hour, and toss together once more just before serving.

CRATES OF FRESHLY PICKED OLIVES (left) *In Tuscany olives are generally hand-picked by workers standing on tall ladders.*

MARBLE KITCHEN (right) *A pot of parsley is left to drain in the marble sink of the villa's cool and elegant kitchen.*

GAMBERI CON I FAGIOLI

Shrimps with Haricot Beans

SERVES 6

300 g (11 oz) dried haricot beans, soaked overnight
in cold water, or canned beans
1 kg (2¼ lb) medium-sized raw shrimps or prawns
salt and freshly milled pepper
1 tablespoon white wine vinegar
1 clove garlic, very finely chopped
2 tablespoons chopped fresh parsley
5 tablespoons olive oil
juice of ½ lemon

Drain the soaked beans, rinse them thoroughly in cold water and put them in a saucepan. Cover with fresh cold water. Bring to the boil and boil very fast for 5 or 6 minutes, then drain and rinse them again. Return them to the saucepan, cover with fresh water and return to the boil. Simmer until tender but not mushy – this takes about 30–40 minutes. (If you are using canned beans, just drain and rinse them gently before using.)

Meanwhile, put the shrimps or prawns into a pan of cold water with a pinch of salt and the vinegar. Bring to the boil and cook until a white foam appears on the surface. Drain them and shell them at once, while they are still hot. Put them to one side.

Drain the cooked beans and put them into a bowl. Add the shrimps or prawns, the garlic, parsley, oil, lemon juice, and salt and pepper to taste. Toss everything together and let stand for about 1 hour. Toss together once more just before serving.

PENNE AL GORGONZOLA

Pasta Quills with Gorgonzola

SERVES 6

200 g (7 oz) ricotta cheese
150 g (5 oz) gorgonzola cheese
4 tablespoons milk
1 small onion, very finely chopped
1 stick celery, very finely chopped
salt and freshly milled pepper
500 g (1 lb 2 oz) pasta quills (penne)

Put the ricotta and the gorgonzola into a food processor or blender with the milk, onion, celery and salt and pepper to taste. Process until quite smooth.

Bring a large pot of salted water to a rolling boil. Toss in the pasta, stir to prevent sticking and boil until *al dente* (check packet for timing as cooking times vary from brand to brand).

Drain the pasta and dress it with the gorgonzola sauce. Toss everything together very thoroughly and serve at once.

CORONA DI RISO CON IL GRANCHIO

Crown of Rice with Crab

SERVES 6

4 tablespoons olive oil
2 cloves garlic
½ dried chilli pepper
500 g (1 lb 2 oz) canned tomatoes, sieved, or
passata
salt
500 g (1 lb 2 oz) brown or white long-grain rice
45 g (1½ oz) butter
750 g (1¾ lb) cooked crab meat, fresh or frozen

Heat the oil, garlic and chilli pepper together in a saucepan for about 5 minutes. Add the tomatoes, stir and partly cover. Simmer for about 15–20 minutes or until reduced.

Meanwhile, bring a large pot of salted water to the boil. Toss in the rice and cook until tender but not mushy. Drain very carefully and return to the saucepan. Add the butter and toss together. Spoon the rice into a 1.3 litre (2¼ pint) metal ring mould, press it down firmly and let it stand for about 4 minutes.

Remove the chilli pepper from the sauce. Add the crab to the tomato sauce and heat through for about 5 minutes. Turn the rice out of the mould on to a large platter, pour the crab and tomato sauce all over the rice crown and serve at once.

CORONA DI RISO CON IL GRANCHIO (left)

POMODORI IN INSALATA CON IL PESTO E I PINOLI

Tomato Salad with Pesto and Pine Kernels

SERVES 6

4 large marmande tomatoes, cut into even slices
2 tablespoons pesto sauce
5 tablespoons olive oil
freshly milled black pepper
2 tablespoons pine kernels
a few fresh basil leaves

Put the sliced tomatoes in a bowl. Mix the pesto and olive oil together and pour it all over the tomatoes. Toss everything together thoroughly. Add freshly milled black pepper to taste and toss again.

Scatter the pine kernels and fresh basil leaves over the salad and then leave it to stand in a cool place until required. Toss the salad again just before serving.

GAMBERI CON I FAGIOLI (above), PARMIGIANA DI ZUCCHINE (below left), ARROSTO DI VITELLO CON PISTACCHI (below right)

ARROSTO DI VITELLO CON PISTACCHI

Pot Roast Veal with Pistachio Nuts

SERVES 6

900 g (2 lb) boned veal joint suitable for roasting
50 g (1¾ oz) pork fat, cut into long strips
25 g (1 oz) shelled, unsalted pistachio nuts
3 sprigs of fresh rosemary
salt and freshly milled pepper
40 g (1½ oz) butter
2 tablespoons olive oil
1 carrot, finely chopped
1 onion, finely chopped
a mixture of fresh or dried herbs: bay leaf, rosemary and sage (if fresh, tie them together with thread so as to be able to remove them easily)
50 ml (1¾ fl oz) brandy
300 ml (½ pint) meat or vegetable stock

Pierce the meat all over with a sharp-pointed knife and insert strips of pork fat, pistachios and rosemary alternately into each hole. When the meat is generously threaded through, season it generously and tie it into shape securely with cook's thread.

Heat the butter and oil in a flameproof casserole and add the vegetables and herbs. Fry until the vegetables are soft, then add the veal joint and seal it all over. Add the brandy and cook for 2–3 minutes until the fumes have evaporated, then add the stock. Cover and simmer for about 20 minutes. Turn the meat over and cook for a further 20 minutes.

Let the meat cool in the casserole, then slice it thinly. Arrange on a platter and serve.

PARMIGIANA DI ZUCCHINE

Courgettes with Tomato, Mozzarella and Parmesan

SERVES 6

6 large courgettes, sliced
300 ml (½ pint) cooking oil for frying
4 tablespoons olive oil
2 cloves garlic, crushed
500 g (1 lb 2 oz) canned tomatoes, sieved
a handful of fresh basil leaves
a large pinch of dried oregano
salt and freshly milled pepper
500 g (1 lb 2 oz) mozzarella cheese, drained and thinly sliced
about 150 g (5 oz) Parmesan cheese, freshly grated

Heat the frying oil until sizzling, then fry the courgettes until golden brown – about 3 minutes each side. Drain and reserve.

Heat the olive oil and garlic together in a saucepan for about 4 minutes without browning the garlic, then add the tomatoes and stir. Add half the basil and the oregano. Season to taste and partly cover. Simmer until reduced and no longer watery – about 10 minutes.

Put a thin layer of the tomato sauce in the bottom of a shallow ovenproof dish. Arrange some slices of fried courgette on top and cover with mozzarella slices, then with a little more tomato sauce. Add a few basil leaves and finish with a generous coating of Parmesan cheese. Repeat until all the ingredients are used up, finishing with a layer of tomato and basil.

Bake in a preheated oven (180°C, 350°F, gas mark 4) for 20–30 minutes or until the mozzarella is melted and stringy. Serve immediately.

BAVARESE AL LAMPONE

Raspberry Bavarois

SERVES 6

500 g (1 lb 2 oz) fresh or frozen raspberries
grated rind and juice of ½ orange
200 g (7 oz) icing sugar, sifted
25 g (scant 1 oz) sheet (or powdered) gelatine
300 ml (½ pint) whipping cream
3 tablespoons caster sugar
olive or almond oil for greasing
raspberries and orange slices for decoration

Push the raspberries through a nylon sieve into a bowl and mix the purée with the orange rind and juice, and icing sugar. Set aside.

Cover the sheet gelatine with cold water and leave to soak for about 10 minutes, then take the sheets out of the water and squeeze them tightly in your fist to dry them. Put the gelatine in a small heatproof bowl or saucepan over a pan of boiling water and allow to melt completely. Strain the gelatine into the berry mixture and stir it all together very thoroughly. Place the bowl in a cool place or on some ice to help it set quickly.

Meanwhile, whip the cream and add the caster sugar. As soon as the berry mixture has begun to set, fold the cream into it with care.

Grease a 1.3 litre (2¼ pt) mould very lightly with oil and spoon the mixture into the mould. Bang the mould down on the work top to settle the contents evenly. Cover and put it in the refrigerator for at least 4 hours.

Dip the mould into boiling water for 5 seconds, then turn the bavarois on to a platter. Decorate with raspberries and orange slices.

LA ZUPPA INGLESE

Italian Trifle

SERVES 6

3 eggs, separated
250 g (8½ oz) caster sugar
50 g (1¾ oz) plain flour, sifted
500 ml (18 fl oz) milk
200 g (7 oz) sponge cake, cut into fingers 5mm (¼ in) thick
25 ml (1 fl oz) rum
25 ml (1 fl oz) of a liqueur of your choice
4 tablespoons chopped mixed candied peel

Beat the egg yolks with 100 g (3½ oz) of the sugar, the flour and 120 ml (4 fl oz) of the milk until smooth. Heat the rest of the milk until just boiling, then stir it into the egg yolk mixture. Return to the heat in the top of a double boiler and cook, stirring constantly, until the custard is thick enough to coat the spoon. Set aside to cool. Whisk the egg whites until stiff, then fold in the remaining sugar. Chill until required.

Lay half of the cake fingers in one plate and the other half in another. Pour the rum over one plate and the liqueur over the other.

In a 30 cm (12 in) ovenproof dish spread a layer of custard, then a layer of cake, a further layer of custard, a sprinkling of candied fruit and so on, until only the whisked egg white is left. Pile this on top of the layered trifle. Bake in a preheated very cool oven (140°C, 275°C, gas mark 1) for about 20 minutes or until golden and crisp. Serve cold.

LADEN BUFFET TABLE *I wanted this party to have a relaxed atmosphere and so let everyone help themselves to the various courses.*

IL COMPLEANNO VENEZIANO DI MARIA

Maria's Venetian Birthday

My friend Maria comes from Venice, and on her birthday we asked another friend who is a professional cook to create for her the ultimate Venetian menu. The results were nothing short of spectacular.

Venetian cooking has two different facets – a simple, homely side in which uncomplicated, filling dishes of vegetables, beans and rice predominate, and a totally contrasting, complex cuisine with more than a hint of ancient splendour and exotic spices from the foreign lands whose ships were once frequent visitors to its port.

The Veneto's most famous dish is, of course, risotto, with countless different combinations of ingredients. I was taught how to make risotto at an early age by a friend of the family who comes from the Veneto area. At the tender age of seven I used to stand on a stool at his elbow and watch him stir and stir, tipping in ladlefuls of stock just at the moment when he told me to do so, and not a second before. As we worked he would tell me the rules: how the rice must be allowed to stick to the bottom a little, how the

surface must ripple like waves, how to let the rice fluff up once it has finished cooking.

For Maria's birthday dinner we dined off antique white lace in a setting which was suitably evocative of a Venetian palazzo, a theme which was taken up in the Doges' soup which began the meal. The amazing purple-red colour of this soup comes from beetroot, which is a fairly unusual ingredient in Italy anyway, but the addition of other vegetables and balls of fried rice make it really very different indeed.

Monkfish is widely used in the Venice area and a stunning dish of monkfish flavoured with fresh mint followed the soup. Another herb, sage, was used in the simple chicken dish which was our main course, accompanied by the ubiquitous Venetian sweet and sour button onions.

As a birthday cake, Maria wanted a classic Venetian cake

POTS AND PANS (left) *Gleaming pots and pans, the legacy of a previous generation of cooks, hang ready for use on the kitchen wall.*

called *fugazza di fichi*. Fugazza is the Venetian word for focaccia, which can mean cake as well as flat pizza bread. There are all kinds of *fugazzas* made in the Veneto area, the most traditional being the *fugazza della Befana*. This very plain cake is traditionally made for Twelfth Night, or 6 January. During this night the old woman Befana is supposed to come down the chimney, bringing presents for all the good children – and sacks of coal for those who have been naughty. So that she finds the cake ready to eat when she comes, the *fugazza* is traditionally wrapped in cabbage leaves then put in the embers of the fire to cook. Maria could remember how the Befana's arrival was prepared for in this way when she was a child and the *fugazza di fichi* reminded her very much of her Venetian childhood.

Menu

Zuppa dei Dogi

Coda di Rospo alla Menta

Cipolline Agrodolce

Pollo alla Salvia

Fugazza di Fichi

DINING ROOM *Our dinner for Maria had a setting evocative of the splendour of a Venetian palazzo.*

ZUPPA DEI DOGI

Doges' Soup

SERVES 6

150 g (5 oz) long-grain white rice
55 g (2 oz) fontina or Edam cheese, grated
½ egg
25 g (1 oz) Parmesan cheese, freshly grated
1 tablespoon olive oil
1.5 litres (2½ pints) clear meat broth
1 large beetroot, boiled, peeled and cut into matchsticks
2 carrots, cut into matchsticks
1 large leek, cut into matchsticks
100 g (4 oz) celeriac, peeled and cut into matchsticks
4–6 tablespoons plain flour
oil for deep frying

Cook the rice in boiling water for about 10 minutes or until still fairly firm in the middle; drain. Mix the rice with the fontina until very well blended, then add the egg, Parmesan and olive oil. Mix very thoroughly. Shape the mixture into walnut-sized balls – you may find you have to squeeze it in your hands so that it sticks together. Chill the balls in the refrigerator until required.

To make the soup, bring the broth to the boil in a large pot, add the vegetable matchsticks and simmer for 10 minutes.

Meanwhile, remove the rice balls from the refrigerator and coat them with flour. (Be sure to handle them carefully so that they do not break up.)

Deep fry in very hot oil until golden. Drain on kitchen paper. Place the rice balls in soup plates and ladle the soup over them. Serve immediately.

PREPARING THE MEAL (left) *The Venetian menu which Alessandro devised was inspired by old and new sources.*

RICE BALLS (below) *Rice dishes, especially superb risottos, figure prominently in Venetian cuisine, and in this soup the deep-fried rice balls add a rich and individual note.*

ZUPPA DEI DOGI (right)

CODA DI ROSPO ALLA MENTA

Minted Monkfish

SERVES *6*

1.3 kg (3 lb) cleaned boneless monkfish
3 tablespoons olive oil
about 10 leaves fresh mint
200 ml (7 fl oz) white wine
2 sachets of saffron powder, or a large pinch of
saffron threads steeped in 2 tablespoons hot water
200 ml (7 fl oz) double cream
salt

After adding the wine and saffron liquid to the
monkfish, simmer for about 15–20 minutes.

Beginning from the tail end, cut the fish into angular wedges. Heat the olive oil in a frying pan with half the mint leaves. Add the monkfish and fry it quickly to seal all sides, turning it over several times to prevent sticking. Add the wine and saffron powder or liquid and simmer for about 15–20 minutes or until the monkfish is tender. Remove the fish from the pan and keep it warm. Add the cream to the pan and simmer to reduce the sauce by about half. Add salt to taste.

Arrange the fish on a warm serving dish and place a fresh leaf of mint between each slice. Discard the mint leaves from the sauce and pour it around the fish. Serve at once.

CODA DI ROSPO ALLA MENTA (below)

SHUTTERED APARTMENT (left) *Even in elegant*
squares the washing still has to be dried.

CIPOLLINE AGRODOLCE

Sweet and Sour Onions

SERVES *6*

24 very large spring onions
50 g (1¾ oz) sugar
75 ml (2½ fl oz) white wine vinegar
330 ml (11 fl oz) water
6–8 cloves
2 bay leaves
10–12 juniper berries
a pinch of salt

Wash and trim the spring onions, removing the green part. Cut the bulbs in half. Put all the other ingredients in a saucepan and boil for 1 minute, then add the onions. Cover and simmer for 10–12 minutes. Serve hot.

POLLO ALLA SALVIA

Sage Chicken

SERVES 6

1 young oven-ready chicken, weighing about 1 kg (2¼ lb), jointed
1 tablespoon cooking oil
1 heaped tablespoon softened butter
200 ml (7 fl oz) dry white wine
50 g (1¾ oz) prosciutto crudo, sliced into thin strips
6–8 fresh sage leaves
salt and freshly milled pepper

Rinse and dry the chicken joints carefully. Heat the oil and butter in a frying pan and brown the chicken joints all over very thoroughly. Drain off most of the fat and add the wine to the pan. Then add the prosciutto crudo and the sage leaves. Season to taste.

Cover and simmer gently until the chicken is cooked through, about 30–40 minutes. Serve at once.

POLLO ALLA SALVIA, *served with green salad.*

FUGAZZA DI FICHI

Venetian Fig Cake

SERVES 8–10

3 eggs
300 ml (½ pint) milk
150 g (5 oz) caster sugar
6 tablespoons Grand Marnier
75 g (2½ oz) butter, softened
400 g (14 oz) plain flour

2 heaped teaspoons baking powder
200 g (7 oz) dried figs, soaked in warm water
for 10 minutes
100 g (3½ oz) raisins, soaked in warm water
for 10 minutes
butter for greasing
flour for dusting
icing sugar for coating

Remove the cake from the tin to cool (below left).
FUGAZZA DI FICHI (below)

Whisk the eggs until completely blended. Add the milk, sugar and Grand Marnier and mix thoroughly. Then add the soft butter and whisk well. Gradually mix in the flour and baking powder. Stir in the drained dried fruit and mix together thoroughly.

Butter and dust with flour a 30 cm (12 in) cake tin. Pour in the cake mixture and smooth the surface. Bake in a preheated moderate oven (180°C, 350°F, gas mark 4) for 40–60 minutes.

Remove the cake from the tin and cool completely on a wire rack. Coat with sifted icing sugar to serve.

IL PRANZO DOMENICALE
IN GIARDINO

Sunday Lunch in the Garden

Every time I go home to Ronchi, in Tuscany, I try to invite my local friends over to catch up on their news and let them know what's happening in my own life. There really is nothing better on a sunny spring day than to sit out under the trees in the garden and eat delicious, simply cooked food with a group of old friends who have a lot of catching up to do.

It is no secret to anyone who knows me just how strongly I feel about this house where I spent much of my childhood. It was here that my passion for good food and wine began. Growing up here meant being involved in a constant bustle around the kitchen, because there never seemed to be fewer than about fifteen people for any meal. As a very small and curious three-year-old, I would peer around the door to see what was happening. Far from being shooed away, I would be greeted gladly and immediately given a job to do – peeling potatoes, shelling peas or scraping barnacles off piles of shiny black mussels. Whatever it was, I was just thrilled to be a part of the whirl of activity.

When it came to the actual meal, I would sit proudly at my end of the table and wait impatiently for the moment when the food would be brought in. I can remember so clearly the warm feeling of immense pride which would wash right over me, knowing that I had had a part in the preparation, however small. I still get the same feeling every time I place a finished dish on the table for family or friends.

On this late spring day we were right in the middle of the strawberry season, so I decided to make a strawberry risotto as a first course. This may sound odd, but in fact risottos made with fruit are quite common and widely appreciated all over Italy these days. The addition of plenty of robust red wine brings out the flavour of the fruit even more acutely. I like it with lots of freshly grated Parmesan sprinkled over the top, but this is a matter of taste.

An early morning trip to the fish market yielded some wonderful dorade, one of my favourite fish, which in spite of its name of gilt-head bream is actually covered in silvery scales. (Red snapper is an alternative for the recipe given here if you cannot find dorade.) The fish was stuffed with fennel and garlic, seasoned, then moistened with olive oil and white wine. Wrapped in foil, it was then baked until tender. From the vegetable garden I picked a huge basketful of lettuce and lots of fresh basil, along with rocket, or arugula, which I love for the distinctive flavour it adds to salads. The dressing was lemon juice and olive oil. This salad and a dish of crispy roast potatoes with lemon and rosemary were the perfect partners for the fish.

One of my favourite combinations is hot and cold foods eaten together and the pudding bore out my theory on how delicious this can be. I made a very lemony soufflé and served it piping hot with a dish of fresh, tangy lemon sorbet. The only complaint to be heard from my guests was that I did not make enough.

LUNCH AL FRESCO (left) *Sunday is the perfect day for a leisurely lunch in the garden to catch up on gossip with old friends.*

Menu

Risotto di Fragole

Orata al Forno con il Finocchio

Patate Arrosto al Limone e Rosmarino

Insalata Verde

Soffiato al Limone

Granita al Limone

FRESH STRAWBERRIES (left) *lend themselves beautifully to a wide variety of dishes, the more unusual strawberry risotto among them.*

RISOTTO DI FRAGOLE

Strawberry Risotto

SERVES 6

55 g (2 oz) unsalted butter
1 small onion, or 2 shallots, finely chopped
500 g (1 lb 2 oz) risotto rice
500 g (1 lb 2 oz) strawberries, hulled
400 ml (14 fl oz) red wine
1 litre (1 ¾ pints) hot chicken or vegetable stock
5 tablespoons double cream
6 tablespoons freshly grated Parmesan cheese
salt and freshly milled black pepper

Melt the butter in a heavy-bottomed saucepan and fry the onion or shallots until soft and translucent. Add the rice and stir to coat it with butter and onion. Slice half the strawberries thinly and stir them into the rice, then add half the wine. Cook until the strawberries become pulpy and the wine is absorbed.

Add the remaining wine and stir to mix. When the wine has been absorbed by the rice, begin to add the hot stock, ladle by ladle. Stir each ladleful of stock into the rice, let it become absorbed and then add more stock. Don't rush this process.

When all the stock has been added and the rice is about 3 minutes from being ready, stir in almost all the remaining strawberries and let them become soft and pulpy. Stir in the cream and Parmesan. Add a little salt and plenty of freshly milled black pepper.

Arrange the risotto on a platter, garnish with the reserved strawberries and serve at once, with extra Parmesan if desired.

ORATA AL FORNO CON IL FINOCCHIO

Baked Dorade with Fennel

SERVES 6

2 dorade (gilt-head bream) or red snapper, weighing
about 1.5 kg (3 ¼ lb) in total, gutted
75 ml (3 fl oz) olive oil
2 large heads of fennel, very thinly sliced
75 ml (3 fl oz) dry white wine
salt and freshly milled pepper
4 cloves garlic, sliced in half

DORADE *It was worth going to the market early for the superbly fresh dorade which were on offer.*

Wash the fish carefully and pat dry. Line an ovenproof dish with foil, leaving enough overlapping to wrap and cover the fish completely but very loosely. Oil the foil lightly on the inside and then lay the fish on top. Stuff the fish with fennel slices, and arrange the remaining fennel under and around the fish. Pour the wine all around the fish. Oil the inside and outside of the fish thoroughly. Sprinkle with salt and pepper, inside and out. Put some of the garlic inside the fish and place the rest around the fish.

Close the foil over the fish and bake in a preheated moderate oven (180°C, 350°F, gas mark 4) for about 1 hour or until the fish is cooked right through. Serve very hot, unwrapping at the table for the best effect.

ORATA AL FORNO CON IL FINOCCHIO *Cooking the fish in foil keeps in all the delicious flavours. When you open the parcel at the table, the aniseed aroma of fennel is released.*

RISOTTO DI FRAGOLE (left)

PATATE ARROSTO AL LIMONE E ROSMARINO

Roast Potatoes with Lemon and Rosemary

SERVES 6

12 medium-sized potatoes, peeled
100 ml (3½ fl oz) olive oil
2 lemons, thickly sliced
a large sprig of rosemary, broken into
small sections
salt
freshly milled pepper

Cut the potatoes in half lengthways and then in half again so as to make segment shapes. Put them into a bowl and pour the oil over them; roll them in the oil with your hands to coat them very thoroughly. Tip the potatoes into a roasting tin and add the lemon slices, putting them underneath the potato segments as much as possible. Put the rosemary sections here and there and season the potatoes generously with salt and pepper.

Place the tin in a preheated hot oven (220°C, 425°F, gas mark 7) and bake for about 50–60 minutes, turning the potatoes over occasionally. When cooked they will be lightly browned and tender all the way through.

INSALATA VERDE

Special Green Salad

SERVES 6

4 hearts of crisp lettuce or 4 'Little Gem' lettuces
a handful of fresh basil leaves
a handful of rocket leaves
8 spring onions, green parts only
2 tablespoons white wine vinegar
½ teaspoon salt
3 cloves garlic, crushed with the side of a knife
½ teaspoon coarse-grain mustard
6–8 tablespoons olive oil
freshly milled black pepper

Shred the lettuce very thinly with a sharp knife. Arrange it on a wide, flattish platter. Tear the basil into pieces and scatter it on the top. Chop the rocket coarsely and scatter it on the lettuce. Slice the green part of the spring onions into small sections and sprinkle this all over the top. Cover the salad and place in the refrigerator until required.

Mix the wine vinegar and salt together until the salt has dissolved, then add the crushed garlic and stir. Add the mustard and stir again, then continue to stir as you pour in the oil. Add freshly milled pepper to taste and let the dressing stand for about 30 minutes before removing the garlic.

Pour the dressing over the salad and toss well. Serve immediately.

SOFFIATO AL LIMONE

Lemon Soufflé

SERVES 6

30 g (1 oz) butter
2 tablespoons plain flour
300 ml (½ pint) milk
grated rind and juice of 2 lemons
6 tablespoons caster sugar
3 egg yolks
4 egg whites
butter for greasing

Melt the butter in a heavy-bottomed pan until foaming. Add the flour and stir until smooth, then add the milk and cook, stirring constantly, until thick. Remove from the heat and mix in the lemon rind and juice, and sugar very thoroughly. Stir in the egg yolks one at a time. Whisk the egg whites until stiff and fold gently into the lemon mixture.

Butter a six-portion soufflé dish very thoroughly, then pour in the lemon mixture. Bake in the centre of a preheated moderately hot oven (190°C, 375°F, gas mark 5) for about 35–40 minutes or until golden and well risen. Serve immediately, alongside the ice-cold sorbet.

GRANITA AL LIMONE

Lemon Sorbet

SERVES 6

250 g (9 oz) caster sugar
600 ml (1 pint) water
grated rind of 1 lemon
juice of 2 lemons

Heat the sugar and water together over a very low heat, stirring, until the sugar has completely dissolved. Then boil gently for 10 minutes until a light syrup has formed. Pour the syrup into a bowl and let it cool completely.

Stir the lemon rind and juice into the syrup. Pour into ice-cube trays (with dividers removed) or other shallow metal trays. Leave for about 40 minutes, until it is half-frozen, then remove and stir thoroughly. Return to the freezer for 2 hours before serving.

SALAD FROM THE GARDEN (opposite left) *The delicious salad of lettuce, basil and rocket leaves was eaten not far from the spot where they had been picked.*

MARKET ON WHEELS (right) *These little pick-ups travel around towns with a loudspeaker to advertise their wares.*

131

LA FESTA DELLA VIGILIA DI NATALE

Christmas Eve Feast

There is a proverb in Italy which says, 'Spend Christmas with your family and Easter with whoever you want.' It underlines the feeling that Christmas is above everything else a time of togetherness, the most important family gathering of the year.

The main Christmas celebration in Italy is on Christmas Eve rather than Christmas Day, and revolves around midnight mass. A great sense of importance is attached to this mass, which is debatedly the second most important in the Catholic calendar. It has social as well as religious importance, however, as this is an occasion for dressing up and being seen – whole families set off for church together in their finery. It is not until they return after midnight that the real Christmas feast begins, with presents exchanged and opened over a long luxurious dinner.

Preparation obviously begins early in the day and the excitement gradually builds up as everyone joins in and the kitchen really starts to bubble with activity. Each member of the family who arrives brings something to add to the already groaning side-

CRIB *At Christmas time many children set up a nativity scene which then decorates the house over the festive period.*

board – someone may turn up with a very special *panettone*, or in our family someone may have detoured via Siena to collect some amazing biscuits and pastries. Presents are already piled under the Christmas tree, closely watched by the children for whom the food that is to come is much less of a concern than the colourfully wrapped gifts. When everything is finally ready, it's time to set the table with the very best tablecloth and china.

Christmas is first and foremost a time for the children, so an attempt is made to give them their supper at around seven o'clock in the evening – although this rarely means that they go to bed and sleep. Some families are very strict and do not allow the children to unwrap a single present until they return from mass. In other families, parents relent and let the little ones open a parcel or two before the adults set off for church. When they eventually return home, it is usually to find the children wide awake and raring to go – this is their present-opening moment!

As you can imagine, the adults may be feeling fairly tired by the time the excited children have at last been packed off to bed. They invariably revive, however, at the thought of the feast to come. The traditional foods for Christmas Eve dinner vary enormously from one area of Italy to the next. As it

is a religious occasion, many families still do not eat meat, but base their meal on fish, with delicious salads and vegetable dishes to accompany it, and all over the country one finds countless local specialities. In Rome, for instance, *capitone*, a giant eel, is served in a marinade of vinegar, bay leaves and garlic; in Calabria, I once had a wonderful Christmas salad called a *mappina*. The sight of shop windows filling up with beautifully decorated boxes of cakes, chocolates and biscuits is a sure sign that Christmas is approaching and while many of them are Sienese in origin, there will be infinite local specialities too.

In recent years, however, the northern European and American tradition of serving poultry at Christmas has gradually been adopted by families throughout Italy, including mine. We certainly kept to tradition as far as our antipasti were concerned, with marinated herrings and paper-thin slices of raw, marinated swordfish to start the meal. To follow, there were freshly made *tortellini in brodo*, pasta hats in a chicken broth, and my aching arms bore witness to the effort I had put into making huge quantities of *tortellini* that afternoon. The alternative was *linguine* with red and black caviar, which looked every bit as good as it tasted. The Veneto area is noted for its excellent poultry dishes and for our main course we

had the wonderfully festive *faraona alla Veronese*, guinea fowl with colourful green peppers.

Italians love desserts and as Christmas is one of *the* times of the year for indulging, the dessert had to be something very special. And it was – literally a mountain of feathery light chestnut purée and whipped cream, with a dusting of chocolate. And of course at Christmas you just have to have a sliver of the deliciously rich *panforte*, or perhaps a slice of light *panettone*. And there is always *pandoro* – a Veronese cake similar to *panettone* – to set off arguments about their relative merits. Everyone eventually mellows, however, over a concluding glass or two of amber-coloured *vin santo*, with perhaps just a little almond-studded Cantucci biscuit to dip in and help it on its way.

Menu

Aringhe Marinate

Carpaccio di Pesce Spada

Linguine al Caviale Rosso e Nero or *Tortellini in Brodo*

Spinaci alla Genovese

Cipolle Arrosto

Faraona alla Veronese

Il Montebianco

Panforte

ARINGHE MARINATE

Marinated Herrings

SERVES 6

12 small (or 6 medium-sized) herrings, gutted and
headless
butter for greasing
1 onion, thinly sliced
2 lemons, thinly sliced
Marinade
30 g (1 oz) butter
120 g (4 oz) carrots, peeled and sliced into rounds
a pinch of dried thyme
a pinch of cayenne pepper
1 bay leaf
1 tablespoon plain flour
500 ml (18 fl oz) dry white wine
3 tablespoons wine vinegar
20 g (¾ oz) salt
1 teaspoon sugar
1 shallot, finely chopped
2 tablespoons chopped fresh parsley
1 teaspoon chopped fresh coriander
a pinch of ground cinnamon
4 cloves
a pinch of dried marjoram

Melt the butter in a pan, add the carrots,
thyme, cayenne and bay leaf and fry until the
carrots are softened but not coloured. Sprinkle
with the flour and stir to brown it lightly, then
pour on the wine and the vinegar, stirring
well. Bring to the boil and boil for 2 minutes.

Add the salt, sugar, shallot, parsley, coriander, cinnamon and cloves and stir to mix
everything together. Simmer the marinade
very gently for about 40 minutes to reduce the
volume of liquid by about one-third.

FISH STALL *Traditionally fish features prominently
in the Christmas Eve menu.*

Wash and dry the herrings carefully and
arrange them in a flameproof dish or pan in a
single layer. Stir the marjoram into the boiling
hot marinade and pour it over the fish. Cover
with a sheet of buttered greaseproof paper.
Place the dish on a very low heat and simmer
for 12 minutes. Remove from the heat and
cool completely.

Arrange the fish carefully on a platter and
cover with the strained marinade. Chill for at
least 24 hours before serving.

Garnish with the sliced onion and lemons,
and serve with plenty of crusty bread.

CARPACCIO DI PESCE SPADA

Swordfish Carpaccio

*Order the slices of swordfish in advance from your
fishmonger. If you are slicing it at home, cut the
swordfish while frozen.*

SERVES 6

12 wafer-thin slices of fresh swordfish
juice of 1 lime
juice of ½ large lemon
salt and freshly milled pepper
250 ml (8 fl oz) olive oil
3 tablespoons chopped fresh parsley

Arrange the fish in a layer in a platter deep
enough to take the oil and juice as well as the
fish. Allow the slices to overlap slightly. Mix
the lime and lemon juices together and add
about ½ teaspoon of salt, though you may
prefer to add more or leave it out altogether.
Stir until the juice has completely dissolved the
salt. Pour this all over the fish in as even a
stream as possible. Turn each slice over to
make sure it is covered completely. Grind
plenty of black pepper on top, then cover the
fish with a layer of olive oil.

Leave the fish slices to marinate for a
minimum of 2 hours, preferably not in the
fridge. If you do refrigerate the dish, make
sure to bring it back to room temperature
before serving.

Just before serving, turn all the slices over to
make sure they are covered in oil on both sides
and sprinkle with the chopped parsley. Serve
with plenty of crusty bread.

LINGUINE AL CAVIALE ROSSO E NERO

Linguine with Red and Black Caviar

SERVES 6

500 g (1 lb 2 oz) linguine, spaghettini, vermicelli
or bavette
salt and freshly milled pepper
75g (2½ oz) unsalted butter
4 tablespoons double cream, Greek yoghurt or
crème fraîche (optional)
1 jar each of red and black caviar (total amount of
caviar must be at least 80 g/2½ oz)

Bring a large pot of salted water to the boil.
Add a large pinch of salt and toss in the pasta.
Stir together quickly to prevent sticking, and
boil until *al dente* – about 7–9 minutes.

Meanwhile, make the caviar sauce. Melt the
butter, without browning it, in a small pan.
Add plenty of freshly milled black pepper and
the cream or yoghurt, if using, and stir quickly
to blend it all together.

Drain the pasta and transfer into a warm
bowl. Remove the sauce from heat, stir in the
caviar and pour the sauce over the drained
pasta. (Do not let the caviar cook or you'll lose
its all too elusive flavour. The beauty of this
dish is its speed!) Toss together quickly and
serve at once.

PASTA

The most widely available and most widely used pasta in Italy is the dry durum wheat variety. Factory made, from just flour and water, it comes in literally hundreds of shapes and sizes and is the staple for Italian cooks in everyday cooking. On special occasions they may turn to fresh pasta, which is actually pasta made with egg and flour. Fresh pasta is sold both dried in packets and soft – in Italy you can buy the latter by weight in a *pastificio*. It is also made at home – for special occasions the rolling pin comes out, the sleeves are rolled up and love, patience and sheer energy are all invested in the resulting pasta.

As well as flour and eggs, salt and olive oil can also be added: salt will make the dough stiffer and oil will make it softer. As you become more expert at making pasta, you will come to know which texture you need, depending on what the pasta is to be used for. For instance, cannelloni need to be made from quite soft dough so they can be rolled easily, whilst the dough for sheets of lasagne should be stiffer; complicated pasta pockets need extremely flexible dough, whereas lasagne should be stiffer; whereas with something easy like tagliatelle it does not really matter.

In making fresh pasta, the most useful thing to have besides a pair of strong arms is a good rolling pin – the long Italian ones are the very best for this purpose. And remember that you will need plenty of space to spread out in if you are making a large quantity. Finally, do keep in mind that fresh egg pasta dries out very quickly, and when dry it is brittle and unmanageable. Do *not* leave it on the work top rolled out and ready to use for any longer than you need to before cutting or filling it.

INGREDIENTS FOR PASTA *With the eggs, add salt or olive oil, depending on how flexible you need the pasta to be.*

You will need the following ingredients:

PER PERSON

100 g (3½ oz) plain flour
1 egg
a pinch of salt (optional)
or
1 teaspoon olive oil (optional)

Put the flour in a pile on the work top and plunge your fist into the middle to make a hole. Break the eggs into the hole and add the

salt or olive oil at this point if using. With your fingers begin to knead everything together very thoroughly, gradually working the flour into the eggs until everything is amalgamated. Then with your hands begin to roll and fold the dough over and over again, until it becomes cool and is smooth and elastic.

Once the dough has reached this stage, begin to roll it out. Roll it out as far as possible, fold it in half, then roll it out again. Repeat this over and over until you hear a slapping sound. This means the air is being pressed out from between the layers and the dough is ready to use.

For *tortellini*, first make the meat filling:

FILLS 200 TORTELLINI

75 g (3 oz) fresh bone marrow
5 tablespoons Parmesan cheese, freshly grated
25 g (1 oz) butter
50 g (2 oz) prosciutto crudo, finely chopped
50 g (2 oz) mortadella, finely chopped
2 egg yolks
a pinch of salt
a pinch of grated nutmeg

Put the bone marrow into a small bowl and place over a pan of warm water to soften the marrow. Remove the bowl from the heat and mash the marrow to a purée with a fork. Add the cheese, butter, prosciutto and mortadella. Stir in the egg yolks and season to taste.

For tortellini, add olive oil to the dough and cut into 4 cm (1½ in) squares. In each square place a very small amount of filling and join two opposite corners to make a triangle. Wrap the triangle around your index finger, folding the two bottom corners in to overlap. Then push the third corner through them to make a rounded pocket shape and push the *tortellino* off with your other hand.

Knead the dough with your fingers until it is smooth and elastic.

Place a tiny amount of meat filling in the centre of each square.

TORTELLINI IN BRODO

Pasta Hats in Chicken Broth

SERVES 6

1 medium-sized oven-ready boiling fowl or 2 kg (4½ lb) chicken
1 large carrot, chopped coarsely
1 large stick celery, chopped coarsely
1 large white onion, studded with 1 clove
2 bay leaves
a handful of fresh parsley
a handful of celery leaves
salt and freshly milled pepper
2.5 litres (4 pints) water
350 g (12½ oz) fresh, ready-made tortellini with a meat filling
freshly grated Parmesan cheese to taste

Put the chicken into a large saucepan with all the vegetables and herbs. Season generously with salt and pepper and cover with the water. Bring to the boil, then cover and simmer for about 2 hours or until the chicken is cooked through and the vegetables are soft.

Remove from the heat, and strain the broth into a large china or glass bowl. Cool completely, then refrigerate overnight.

Skim the fat off the surface of the chilled broth and strain the broth again into a large saucepan. Reheat the broth slowly and bring it to the boil. Toss in the tortellini and stir gently so they don't split. Cook for about 4–5 minutes, until they are cooked through.

Transfer the soup to a tureen and serve steaming hot with plenty of freshly grated Parmesan cheese offered separately.

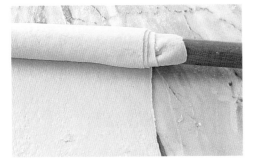

Roll out the dough over and over again – it helps to have a long rolling pin.

Fold in the corners of the squares to make rounded pasta pockets.

SPINACI ALLA GENOVESE

Spinach with Raisins and Pine Kernels

SERVES 8

2 kg (4½ lb) fresh spinach, washed and trimmed
100 g (3½ oz) butter
100 g (3½ oz) raisins, soaked in warm water for
10 minutes
100 g (3½ oz) pine kernels
salt

Steam the spinach for about 4 minutes or until half cooked. Drain it carefully and squeeze out any remaining water with your hands.

Melt the butter in a large pan, add the spinach and mix together using 2 forks. Drain the raisins and add them to the spinach, followed by the pine kernels. Mix all together, add salt to taste and serve at once.

CIPOLLE ARROSTO

Roast Onions

SERVES 8

8 medium-sized, even-shaped red onions
1 egg
5 tablespoons freshly grated Parmesan cheese
2 tablespoons brandy
salt and freshly milled pepper
2 tablespoons fresh breadcrumbs
30 g (1 oz) butter
4 tablespoons olive oil

Drop the onions into a pot of boiling water and leave them there for about 2 minutes. Remove them with a slotted spoon and peel them quickly. Cut the top and bottom off each one and press out the heart from inside each onion to create a hollow. Chop the hearts finely and put them in a small bowl with the egg. Add the Parmesan cheese, brandy, and salt and pepper to taste. Stir thoroughly. Mix in the breadcrumbs. Spoon this mixture into the hollow created inside each onion.

Butter an ovenproof dish and sit the stuffed onions in the dish in neat rows. Brush with oil and dot with butter. Cover loosely with foil and bake in a preheated moderately hot oven (190°C, 375°F, gas mark 5) for about 45 minutes to 1 hour or until the onions are tender all the way through.

SHELLING PINE NUTS (left) *Pine nuts are extracted from the cones of the umbrella pine and getting at the kernels can be hard work.*

FARAONA ALLA VERONESE (above), *and served with a slice of fried polenta* (below).

FARAONA ALLA VERONESE

Veronese Guinea Fowl

SERVES 6–8

2 small oven-ready guinea fowl, jointed
2 tablespoons plain flour
a large pinch of salt
3 tablespoons sunflower oil
200 ml (6 fl oz) dry white wine
300 ml (½ pint) chicken stock, kept hot
3 red peppers
250 g (9 oz) celeriac, peeled and cut into cubes
5 tablespoons Grand Marnier
100 g (3 ½ oz) sultanas, soaked in warm water for 10 minutes

Carefully trim some of the fat off the guinea fowl joints. Mix the flour and salt together and coat the joints, shaking off any excess. Heat the oil in a large frying pan and fry until golden brown all over. Drain on kitchen paper and transfer to a flameproof baking dish.

Add the wine and about 2 ladlefuls of the stock to the dish and cook covered on top of the stove for 25 minutes on a low heat. Meanwhile, bring a large pot of water to the boil, toss in the peppers and blanch for about 4 minutes. Drain, then cut into 2.5 cm (1 in) squares and set aside. Cook the celeriac in boiling salted water until tender; drain.

Warm the Grand Marnier, pour over the guinea fowl and flame it. Arrange the peppers and celeriac around the guinea fowl. Drain the sultanas and add them to the dish, with a little more stock to cover the ingredients. Cover and cook in a preheated oven (180°C, 350°F, gas mark 4) for 10–12 minutes. Serve hot on a large platter.

IL MONTEBIANCO

The Mont Blanc

SERVES 5–6

750 g (1¾ lb) fresh chestnuts
2 tablespoons boiling hot milk
1 teaspoon vanilla essence
150 g (5 oz) icing sugar, sifted
1 tablespoon brandy
300 ml (½ pint) whipping cream
(sweetened to taste)
1 teaspoon unsweetened cocoa powder

Put the chestnuts in a saucepan, cover with cold water and bring to the boil. Cook until tender. Peel them quickly whilst still hot so that the inner brown skin comes away easily. Push the still hot chestnuts through a mouli on a very fine setting. Mix the resulting purée *lightly* with a fork.

Stir the milk, vanilla essence, sugar and brandy together and stir this *lightly* into the chestnut purée. Push this mixture through a mouli on the finest setting, letting it fall on to a platter in a mountain shape. Whip the cream. Cover the mountain *lightly* with the cream, dust with cocoa powder around the base and serve at once, or chill until required.

You are aiming for lightness of texture, so be careful how you handle these ingredients! An alternative is to cover the dish on to which you will build the cake with a layer of crushed meringues. For this quantity, use about 5 fist-sized meringues, broken into pieces.

IL MONTEBIANCO (left), PANFORTE (right)

CANDIED FRUITS (right) *Candied fruits and peel are used in many Christmas specialities.*

PANFORTE

Sienese Sweetmeat

For authenticity, candied popone should be used in this sweetmeat, but if you can't get hold of it, use candied peel.

MAKES ONE 20 CM (8 IN) CAKE

200 g (7 oz) shelled almonds
120 g (4 oz) shelled walnuts
280 g (10 oz) plain flour

300 g (11 oz) candied peel, finely chopped
a pinch each of ground cinnamon, ground coriander, ground cloves and grated nutmeg
300 g (11 oz) caster sugar
rice paper
extra 2 teaspoons ground cinnamon

Blanch the almonds and the walnuts separately in boiling water. Remove the skins then chop or grind the nuts separately into a fine powder.

Set aside about 3 tablespoons of flour. Mix the remaining flour with the chopped candied peel. Stir in the chopped almonds, then the chopped walnuts and then the spices.

Put the sugar in a very small heavy-bottomed saucepan with just enough water to dampen it. Heat until you achieve a 'rubbery' texture, not a syrup. Mix this into the rest of the ingredients and stir thoroughly.

Line a 20 cm (8 in) shallow cake tin with rice paper. Spread the nut mixture in the tin. Sprinkle over the reserved flour mixed with the 2 teaspoons of cinnamon. Bake in a preheated moderately hot oven (190°C, 375°F, gas mark 5) for about 30 minutes. Shake off the loose flour and cinnamon from the top, and cool the cake before serving. (It will remain flat and unrisen.)

INDEX

A

abbachio a scottadito 57
agnello braciato 19
albanesi 31
Albanian biscuits 31
albicocche ripiene di ricotta e noci 74
almond and ricotta filling 74
    jelly 101
amaretto tart, plum jam and 38
anchovies, bread and figs 45
    pizza 89
antipasti 133
apricots in red wine 45
    with almond and ricotta filling
    74
aringhe marinate 134
arrosto di vitello con pastacchi 115
artichokes in mixed vegetables 81
    torta pasqualina 21
    with peas 13
asparagi alla Milanese 64–5
asparagus, Milanese 64–5
aubergines, chicken with 97
    salad, fried 95

B

bacon, mussel kebabs with 56
bananas, chocolate 61
banane al cioccolato 61
bavarese al lampone 116
béchamel sauce 66
beef fillet with mixed vegetables
    81
    hamburgers with chilli 57
    Italian hamburgers 57
    kebabs 59
    minced, and chicken liver puree
    79
    pizzaiola 36
biscuits, Albanian 31
branzino al sale 82
bread and tomato salad 74
    baked dry, with cheese 26
    figs and anchovies 45
    see also focaccia, toast

bream *see* dorade
broad beans purée 19
broccoli and pasta soup 26
brodo di pesce 10
broth, chicken 137
    fish 10
bruschetta 61
bucatini with sardines 105
budino di ricotta 89
'burn your fingers' lamb cutlets 57

C

cabbage leaves, stuffed 27
cakes, Easter dove 22
    panforte 141
    rice 39
    Sicilian cassata 90
    traditional Neapolitan Easter 15
    Venetian fig 125
Calabria 133
calzone 89
cannelloni ripieni di ricotta e salsicce
    87
    with ricotta and sausage filling
    87
canneli alla Siciliana 85
capellini pasta nests 50
capesante gratinate 78
cappuccio imbottito 27
carciofi e pisellini alla Romana 13
carote al latte 21
carpaccio di pesce spada 134
carrots in milk 21
cassata alla Siciliana 85, 90
    gelata alla Siciliana 98
caviar, linguine with 135
cazzilli 98
celery with gorgonzola 73
cheese and potato filling for
    ravioli 88
    baked dry bread with 26
    pie 74
    see also specific types
cherry ice cream, mangoes with
    107
chestnuts: Mont Blanc 140
chicken broth 137
    liver and minced beef purée 79
    sage 124

salad 43
    with aubergines 97
chocolate bananas 61
    cassata cake 90
Christmas Eve 133
cinnamon jelly 53
Cinqueterre 70
cipolle arrosto 139
cipolline agrodolce 123
cod, baked baby 48
coda di rospa alla menta 123
coffee sorbet with whipped cream
    101
columba, la 17, 22
corona di riso con il granchio 114
cotolette di tacchino 72
courgettes deep-fried, and their
    flowers 65
    risotto 71
    with tomato, mozzarella and
    Parmesan 116
crab with rice 114
crespelle di ricotta e spinaci 66
crostata di marmellata 38
    di ricotta 90
crostini alla Toscana 79
culigiones 88
custard filling for flan 90

D

Doges' soup 120
dorade, baked, with fennel 127,
    129
    with olives 9, 12
dressing, balsamic vinegar 36

E

Easter cake 15
    dove cake 17, 22
    eggs 17
Easter Sunday 17
eggs, ricotta with 89
    see also omelette

F

falsomagro al sugo 51
faraona alla veronese 139
fave in purè 19
fegato alla veneziana 35

fennel with baked dorade 129
Festa della Donna 46
fichi verdi con zabaglione di prosecco
    69
fig cake, Venetian 125
    bread, anchovies and 45
filetti di sogliola all'arancia 13
fiori di zucchini 65
fish broth 10
    casserole with olives 97
    ravioli 8, 11
    see also shellfish *and specific types*
flan, ricotta 90
focaccia con peperoni 72
    with braised peppers 72
fragoline al vino bianco 83
frittata del Venerdí Santo 8, 11
    di cipolla 42
fugazza della Befana 119
    di fichi 125

G

gamberi con i fagioli 114
    in intingolo 106
gelatina di mandorle 101
gelato all'amarena con il mango 107
gelo di cannella 51
Giulia's rice cake 39
Good Friday 8–9
    omelette 8, 11
gorgonzola, pasta quills with 114
grande minestrone vegetale 35
granita al limone 131
    di caffè con panna 101
gratin of scallops 78
green figs with prosecco
    zabaglione 69
guinea fowl, Veronese 139

H

hamburger all'Italiana 57
    piccanti 57
    with chilli 57
haricot beans, shrimps with 114
herrings, marinated 133, 134

I

ice cream cassata 98
    cherry 107

insalata di pollo 43
   mozzarella, olive e rucola 112
   verde 130
insalatina all'aceto balsamico 36
Italian barbecued toast 61
   hamburgers 57
   trifle 116

J
jelly, almond 101
   cinnamon 53

K
kebabs, beef 59
   lamb 58
   mussel 56
kid 17
kidneys, grilled lamb's 30

L
lamb 17
   braised 19
   cutlets, 'burn your fingers' 57
   grilled kidneys 30
   kebabs with green peppers 58
langoustines, roasted 104
lasagnette con spinaci e funghi 18
   with spinach and mushrooms 18
lemon sorbet 131
   soufflé 130
Leopard's timbale 48
Ligurian Easter pie 17, 21
linguine al caviale rosse e nero 135
   with red and black caviar 135
liver and onions 35

M
macaroni: Leopard's timbale 48
mackerel cooked in Palermo style 106
maltagliati al sugo di pomodoro 28-9
   with tomato sauce 28-9
mangoes with cherry ice cream 107
mascarpone con le pere 45
   tiramisú 83
   with pears 45
meat filling for tortellini 136

melanzane fritte in insalata 95
Milan 62, 76
Milanese asparagus 64-5
minced meat: stuffed cabbage leaves 27
minestra di pasta e broccoli 26
minestrone 35
minted monkfish 123
Molise 86
monkfish, minted 123
Mont Blanc 140
montebianco, il 140
mozzarella, baked dry bread with 26
   con verdura mista 42
   courgettes, tomato and Parmesan 116
   in carrozza 68
   salad with black olives and rocket 112
   with mixed vegetables 42
mushrooms, lasagnette with spinach and 18
   with stewed octopus 106
mussel kebabs 56

N
Name Days 33
Naples 9
nasello al gratin 48
   alla Palermitana 106
Neapolitan Easter cake 15
nidi di scuma 59
nuts: panforte 141

O
octopus, stewed, with mushrooms 106
olive nere marinate 34
olives and fish casserole 97
   baked dorade with 12
   black, mozzarella and rocket salad 112
   marinated black 34
omelette, flat onion 42
   Good Friday 8, 11
onions and steak pie 48
   liver and 35
   omelette 42

roast 139
   sweet and sour 123
oranges with sardines, Sicilian 94
orata al forno con il finocchio 129
   alle olive 9, 12

P
pancakes, ricotta and spinach 66
pandoro 133
pane fichi e alici 45
panforte 141
panzanella, la 74
parmaoiana di zucchine 116
parmesan, courgettes, tomato and mozzarella 116
Pasqua, la 17
pasta 136-7
   and broccoli soup 26
   hats in chicken broth 137
   nests fried 50
   quills with gorgonzola 114
   with sardines 105
   see also specific types
pastiera, la 9, 15
patate arrosto 20
   al limone e rosmarino 129
peach dessert, frozen 99
   in red wine 45
pears in red wine 45
   mascarpone with 45
peas with artichokes 13
penne al gorgonzola 114
peperoni al ferri 60
   arrosto 95
peppers, braised, focaccia with 72
   green, lamb kebabs with 58
   grilled 60, 95
pesce alla matalotta 97
pesche al vino 45
pesto, pine kernels and tomato salad 115
pezzelle di pane 26
pick me up 83
pies: Leopard's timbale 48
   Ligurian Easter 21
   savoury 74
pine kernels, pesto and tomato salad 115
   spinach with raisins and 138

pistachio nuts with pot roast veal 115
pizza, stuffed 89
pizzaiola, la 36
plum jam and amaretto tart 38
pollo alla cacciatora con melanzane 97
   alla salvia 124
polpetti in umido con funghi 106
pomodori in insalata con il pesto e i pinoli 115
potatoes and cheese filling for ravioli 88
   fritters, Sicilian 98
   mashed, with lemon 36
   roast 20
prawns, stewed 106
pudding, ricotta 89
purè di patate al limone 36
purée of broad beans 19
   of beef and chicken liver 79

R
radicchio al ferri 59
   grilled 59
raisins, spinach with pine kernels and 138
raspberry bavarois 116
ravioli di pesce 8, 11
   Sardinian 88
red snapper baked with fennel 129
reef spaghetti 79
rice cake 39
   Doges' soup 120
   with crab 114
ricotta 85-6
   and almond filling 74
   and sausage filling 87
   and spinach pancakes 66
   cassata cake 90
   flan 90
   in canape 89
   pudding 89
   with eggs 89
risotto, con zucchine e fiori 81
   di fragole 128
   Milanese asparagus 64-5
   strawberry 128
   with courgettes and their flowers 81

rocket, mozzarella and black olive
    salad 112
rognone di vitello alla furnacella 30
Roman artichokes with peas 13
Rome 8-9, 133

S
sage chicken 124
Saint Giuseppe 33
salad, chicken 43
    fried aubergine 95
    leaves with balsamic vinegar
        dressing 36
    mozzarella with black olives
        and rocket 112
    special green 130
    tomato and bread 74
    tomato with pesto and pine
        kernels 115
sarde a beccafico 94
sardines with oranges, Sicilian
    94
    with pasta 105
Sardinian ravioli 88
sauce, béchamel 66
    Syracuse 105
    tomato 29, 87
sausage and ricotta filling for
    cannelloni 87
savoury pie 74
scallops, gratin of 78
scampi arrosto 104

sea bass baked in salt 82
sedano con il gorgonzola 73
shellfish spaghetti 79
    see also mussels; shrimps
shrimps with haricot beans 114
Sicilian cassata cake 90
    potato fritters 98
    sardines with oranges 94
    stuffed meat roll 51
Sicily 46, 55, 85, 93
Siena 133
Sienese sweetmeat 141
soffiato al limone 130
sole fillets with orange 13
sorbet, lemon 131
soup, broccoli and pasta 26
    Doges' 120
    vegetable minestrone 35
spaghetti aglio e olio 42
    allo scoglio 79
    reef 79
    with oil and garlic 42
spiedini d'agnello con peperone 58
    di cozze 56
    di manzo 59
spinach and ricotta pancakes 66
    lasagnette with mushrooms and
        18
    with raisins and pine kernels
        138
spinaci alla genovese 138
spuma gelata di pesche 99

steak and onion pie 48
strawberries: risotto 128
    wild, with white wine 83
stuffed cabbage leaves 27
    meat roll 51
    pizza 89
sweet and sour onions 123
sweetmeat, Sienese 141
swordfish carpaccio 134

T
tagliata vegetariana 81
tart, plum jam and amaretto
    38
timballo del gattopardo 46, 48
tiramisù 83
toast, Italian barbecued 61
    Tuscan 79
tomato and bread salad 74
    courgettes, mozzarella and
        Parmesan 116
    salad with pesto and pine
        kernels 115
    sauce 28-9, 87
torta di riso di Giulia 39
    pasqualina, la 17, 21
    salata 74
tortellini 136
    in brodo 137
trifle, Italian 116
turkey escalopes 72
Tuscan toast 79

Tuscany 40, 55, 76, 111, 127
Twelfth Night 119

V
veal pot roast, with pistachio nuts
    151
    stuffed meat roll 51
vegetables: fried pasta nests 50
    mixed with beef fillet 81
    mixed, mozzarella with 42
    soup 120
    see also specific vegetables
Venerdì santo 8-9
Venetian fig cake 125
    liver and onions 35
Veneto 118, 133
Venice 118
vermicelli with sauce of Syracuse
    105
Veronese guinea fowl 139
vin santo 133
vinegar dressing, balsamic 36

W
whiting, baked 48
    cooked in Palermo style 106

Z
zabaglione, green figs with
    prosecco 69
zuppa dei Dogi 120
    inglese 116

ACKNOWLEDGMENTS

Valentina Harris and Conran Octopus would like to thank the following people for their help:
Giulia dell'Amico, Beppino and Andreina de Battisti, Eleonora Carpi, Eleonora Consoli (Catania), Katia Fongoli, Aldo di Maria (Palermo), Ferruccio Nobile Migliore, Conte and Contessa Notabartolo (Catania), Maria-Teresa Olcese (Milano), Cristina Pagani (Milano), Gerardo and Cetty Rossano (Palermo), Salvatore Rubino (Palermo), Howard, Linda, Lucia and Benedetta Scott and friends, Nicholas and Daniel.

For front jacket photography styling: Jane Newdick
For front jacket photography art direction: Georgina Rhodes